Block Trace Analysis and Storage System Optimization

A Practical Approach with MATLAB/Python Tools

Jun Xu

Apress®

Block Trace Analysis and Storage System Optimization: A Practical Approach with MATLAB/Python Tools

Jun Xu
Singapore, Singapore

ISBN-13 (pbk): 978-1-4842-3927-8   ISBN-13 (electronic): 978-1-4842-3928-5
https://doi.org/10.1007/978-1-4842-3928-5

Library of Congress Control Number: 2018964058

Managing Director, Apress Media LLC: Welmoed Spahr
Acquisitions Editor: Susan McDermott
Development Editor: Laura Berendson
Coordinating Editor: Rita Fernando

Cover designed by eStudioCalamar

Cover image designed by Freepik (www.freepik.com)

Distributed to the book trade worldwide by Springer Science+Business Media New York, 233 Spring Street, 6th Floor, New York, NY 10013. Phone 1-800-SPRINGER, fax (201) 348-4505, e-mail orders-ny@springer-sbm.com, or visit www.springeronline.com. Apress Media, LLC is a California LLC and the sole member (owner) is Springer Science + Business Media Finance Inc (SSBM Finance Inc). SSBM Finance Inc is a **Delaware** corporation.

For information on translations, please e-mail rights@apress.com, or visit www.apress.com/rights-permissions.

Apress titles may be purchased in bulk for academic, corporate, or promotional use. eBook versions and licenses are also available for most titles. For more information, reference our Print and eBook Bulk Sales web page at www.apress.com/bulk-sales.

Any source code or other supplementary material referenced by the author in this book is available to readers on GitHub via the book's product page, located at www.apress.com/9781484239278. For more detailed information, please visit www.apress.com/source-code.

Printed on acid-free paper

To Grace, Alexander, and Arthur.

Table of Contents

About the Author

Jun Xu got his BS in Mathematics and a PhD in Control from Southeast University (China) and Nanyang Technological University (Singapore), respectively. He is a Lead Consultant Specialist at Hongkong-Shanghai Banking Corporation (HSBC) and was a Principal Engineer at Western Digital. Before that, he was with Data Storage Institute, Nanyang Technological University, and National University of Singapore for research and development. He has multi-discipline knowledge and solid experience in complex system modeling and simulation, data analytics, data center, cloud storage, and IoT. He has published over 50 international papers, 15 US patents (applications), and 1 monograph. He is an editor of the journal *Unmanned Systems* and was a committee member of several international conferences. He is a senior member of IEEE and a certificated FRM.

About the Technical Reviewers

Yunpeng Chai received BE and PhD degrees in Computer Science and Technology from Tsinghua University in 2004 and 2009, respectively. He is currently an Associate Professor at the School of Information at Renmin University of China and Vice Dean of the department of Computer Science and Technology. His research interests include SSD/NVM-based hybrid storage systems, distributed key-value stores, and cloud storage virtualization. He regularly publishes in prestigious journals and conferences (like IEEE Transactions on Parallel and Distributed Systems, IEEE Transactions on Computers, MMST, etc.). He is a member of the Information Storage Technology Expert Committee in the China Computer Federation.

Li Xia is an Associate Professor at the Center for Intelligent and Networked Systems (CFINS), Department of Automation, Tsinghua University, Beijing China. He received his BS and PhD degrees in Control Theory in 2002 and 2007, respectively, both from Tsinghua University. After graduation, he worked at IBM Research China as a research staff member (2007–2009) and at the King Abdullah University of Science and Technology (KAUST) in Saudi Arabia as a postdoctoral research fellow (2009–2011). Then he returned to Tsinghua University in 2011. He was a visiting scholar at Stanford University, the Hong Kong University of Science and Technology, etc. He serves/served as an associate editor and program committee member of a number of international journals and conferences.

His research interests include the methodology research in stochastic learning and optimization, queuing theory, Markov decision processes, reinforcement learning, and the application research in storage systems, building energy, energy Internet, industrial Internet, Internet of Things, etc. He is a senior member of IEEE.

Acknowledgments

A major component of this work came as a result of my 16 years of R&D experience on data analytics and storage systems at Western Digital, Temasek Labs, and Data Storage Institute. I would like to acknowledge Western Digital for allowing me to publish some of my job-related work. During the preparation of this book, I received support and advice from many friends and colleagues. Here I only mention few: Dr. Jie Yu, Dr. Guoxiao Guo, Robin O'Neill, Grant Mackey, Dr. Jianyi Wang, David Chan, Wai-Ee Wong, Dr. Yi Li, Samuel Torrez, Shihua Feng, Jiang Dan, Terry Wu, Allen Samuels, Gregory Thelin, William Boyle, David Hamilton, John Clinton, Nils Larson, Karanvir Singh, Eric Lee, and Sang Huynh. In particular, Junpeng Niu, my PhD student and colleague, also helped me with a few paragraphs in Chapter 1 on hybrid disks.

I would also like to thank the technical reviewers, Yunpeng Cai and Li Xia, for their very helpful comments. Deep appreciation also goes out to the editors, Susan McDermott, Rita Fernando, Laura Berendson, Amrita Stanley, Krishnan Sathyamurthy and Joseph Quatela for their hard work.

Last but not least, I am most grateful to my wife, Grace, for the love and encouragement provided through my entire life, and to my two boys, Alexander and Arthur, who remind me that there is a life beyond the work. Without their great patience and enthusiastic support, I would not have been able to complete this book.

Introduction

In the new era of IoT, big data, and cloud systems, better performance and higher density of storage systems become more crucial in many applications.

To increase data storage density, new techniques have evolved, including shingled magnetic recording (SMR), heat-assistant magnetic recording (HAMR) for HDD, 3D Phase Change Memory (PCM) and Resistive RAM (ReRAM) for SSD. Furthermore, some hybrid and parallel access techniques together with specially designed IO scheduling and data migration algorithms have been deployed to develop high performance data storage solutions.

Among the various storage system performance analysis techniques, IO event trace analysis (block-level trace analysis in particular) is one of the most common approaches for system optimization and design. However, the task of completing a systematic survey is challenging and very few works on this topic exist. Some books provide theoretical fundamentals without enough practical analysis in physical systems, and others discuss the performance of some specific storage systems without proposing a tool that can be applied widely.

To fill this gap, this book brings together IO properties and metrics, trace parsing, and result reporting perspectives, based on MATLAB and Python platforms. It provides self-inclusive content on block-level trace analysis techniques, and it includes typical case studies to illustrate how these techniques and tools can be applied in real applications such as SSHD, RAID, Hadoop, and Ceph systems.

This book starts with an introduction in Chapter 1, which provides the background of data storage systems and general trace analysis. I show that the wide applications of block storage devices motivate the intensive study of various block-level workload properties.

Chapter 2 gives an overview of traces, in particular, the block-level traces. After introducing the common workload properties, I discuss the trace metrics in two categories, the basic ones and the advanced ones.

In Chapter 3, I present the ways to collect the block-level trace in both hardware and software tools. In particular, I show how the most popular tool in Linux system, blktrace, works in a simple setting.

In Chapter 4, I investigate the design of trace analyzers. I discuss the interactions of the workload with system components, algorithms, structure, and applications.

Case study is the best way to learn the methodology and the corresponding tools. This book will provide some examples to show how the analysis can be applied to real storage system tuning, optimization, and design. Therefore, from Chapter 5 to Chapter 9, I provide some typical examples for trace analysis and system optimization.

Chapter 5 presents the properties of traces from some benchmark tools, such as SPC and PCMarks. I show how to capture the main characteristics and then formulate a "synthetic" trace generator. I also show how the cache is affected by the workload, and how a proper scheduling algorithm is designed.

Chapter 6 attempts to explain the mystery behind SSHD's performance boost in SPC-1C under WCD (write cache disabled). I show from the trace how a new hybrid structure can help to improve system performance.

Chapter 7 discusses the trace under two RAID systems with different read and write properties. I illustrate that the parity structure has a big impact on the overall performance.

Chapter 8 first reviews the literature on Hadoop workload analysis. And then I discuss the WD Hadoop cluster in a production environment. After that, the workload properties are analyzed, in particular, for SMR drives.

Chapter 9 analyzes the Ceph system performance. Storage and the CPU/network/memory are discussed. I show that these components shall be considered as a unified system in order to identify the performance bottleneck.

The tools used in the book are introduced in the appendix. I first introduce the tool based on MATLAB. Then, I show how this tool is converted into the Python platform.

CHAPTER 1

Introduction

The chapter provides the background of data storage systems and general trace analysis. I will show that wide applications of block storage devices motivate the intensive study of various block-level workload properties. I will also list the objectives and contributions of this book in this chapter.

Basics of Storage

In this information-rich world, data storage devices and systems are fundamental for information preservation. There are so many different types of storage devices available in the market, such as magnetic tape, optical disc drive, hard disk drive (HDD), solid state drive (SSD), flash memory, etc. Historically, there were even more types, like twister memory and drum memory. To narrow the focus, I will cover the modern computer storage/memory devices only. They can be generally divided into two categories [1].

- Volatile
    - The commonly used, such as DRAM (dynamic RAM), SRAM (static RAM), etc.
    - Those under development: T-RAM (thyristor RAM), Z-RAM (zero-capacitor), etc.

© Jun Xu 2018
J. Xu, *Block Trace Analysis and Storage System Optimization*,
https://doi.org/10.1007/978-1-4842-3928-5_1

- Non-volatile

  - ROM (read-only memory), such as EPROM
    (Erasable Programmable ROM), EEPROM
    (Electrically E-PROM), MROM (Mask ROM), etc.

  - NVRAM, such as flash memory, PCM (phase
    change memory), ReRAM/RRAM (resistive
    RAM), MRAM (magnetoresistive RAM), FeRAM
    (ferroelectric RAM), etc.

  - Mechanical devices like HDD, magnetic tape,
    optical disc drives

When selecting a storage device or system, many factors must be considered carefully, such as price, performance, capacity, power efficiency, reliability, data integrity, durability, form factor, operating temperature, connection types, and so on, depending on the application scenarios. However, the performance of the devices is the major topic of this book.

Storage Devices

In this section, I discuss several types of non-volatile storage devices, as some volatile devices like RAM, will be used inside those non-volatile devices as cache.

HDD

HDD was first introduced by IBM in 1956. Soon it became the dominant secondary storage device for general purpose computers. Even now, it is still the mainstream storage device, in particular for data centers. Despite the fact that disk drives are commodity products today, a disk drive is an extremely complex electromechanical system encompassing decades of finely honed research and development on an immense multitude of diverse disciplines, although the main components of the modern HDD have remained basically the same for the past 30 years. Figure 1-1[1] shows the components as assembled, and Figure 1-2 illustrates the basic electronics blocks.

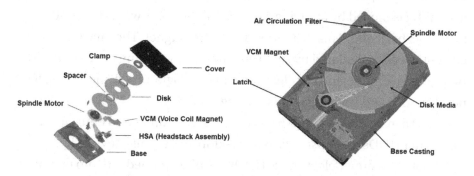

Figure 1-1. *Basic components of a HDD*

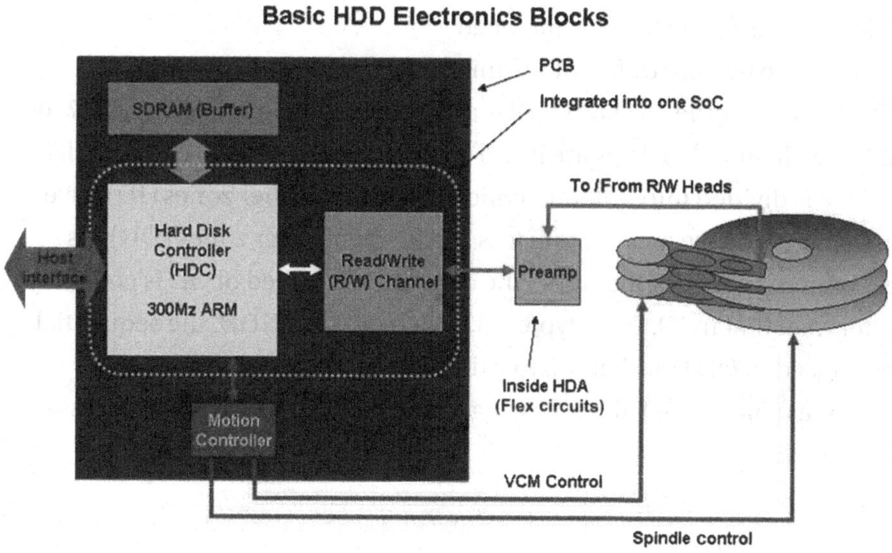

Basic HDD Electronics Blocks

Figure 1-2. *Basic HDD electronics blocks*

---

[1]All figures are provided in the source code download file for this book. To access the source code, go to www.apress.com/9781484239278 and click the Download Source Code button.

In particular, the servo is one of the most precise mechanical systems in the world. The disk head that reads and writes data to the medium is only few nanometers above the disc media; this is similar to a Boing 737 plane flying a few meters above the ground. The HSA (head stack assembly) is moved by applying a current to the wires wound around a loop at its back end. This coil forms an electromagnet. The amount of current used is calculated by servo electronics. By varying the current, very precise acceleration and deceleration can be programmed, increasing IO performance and servo head positioning accuracy.

HDD can be divided into two categories: consumer and enterprise. Consumer HDDs are mostly used in desktop and mobile devices like a notebook. Consumer electronics HDDs are often embedded into digital video recorders, smart TVs, and automotive vehicles. Enterprise HDDs usually have higher reliability than consumer HDDs, with higher quality requirements for the media and head.

Disk drives have different spinning speeds (rotation per minute, RPM). For example, desktop HDDs are usually in 3.5-inch form with 7200 RPM, while mobile HDDs are in 2.5-inch form with 5400 RPM. Each disc surface is divided into different concentric zones. Inner zones (ID) have less physical space and contain less sectors than outer zones (OD). As the spinning speed is the same, the data transfer speed of OD is generally faster than that in ID. For a typical 3.5-inch desktop HDD, the sequential read speed in OD could be 1.5 to 2 times than that in ID.

For a typical HDD, the following formula calculates average access time (T_a) [2, 3]:

$$T_a = T_s + T_l + T_t + T_o \tag{1.1}$$

where

- Seek time as T_s: Time required to move the heads a desired distance. Typically specified at 1/3 the radius of the platter. The settle time is generally included in this part.

- Rotational latency as T_l: Amount of time the drive must wait before data is under the read/write head.

- Transfer time as T_t: Amount of time required to transfer data to or from the host.

- Controller overhead as T_o: How long it takes the drive to decode a command from the host.

Note that the read head is usually different from the write head, and the internal firmware process for reads and writes is also different. So there will be a slight variance for read and write seek times. Usually, write access costs more because of the longer setting time of a write, which is caused by PES (position error signal) requirement, which means write access requires a stronger condition on PES than read access. By design, faster RPM drives have faster average access times than slower RPM drives due to shorter latency and seek times.

The response time (T_{res}) is a different concept from the access time. In fact, since the conventional disk drive can only process one request at one time, some incoming requests have to wait in a queue. For example, some write requests may be buffered in DRAM write cache first and must wait for the previous request to be completed. Note that although there are many arms and heads per drive, the arms must move together since there is only one VCM to drive them in general. Thus,

$$T_{res} = T_a + T_w \qquad (1.2)$$

where T_w is the waiting or queueing time just after the request enters the queue and before it is actually executed.

Owning to the influence of the command queue, cache has large impact on the performance of both read and write. Thus, a large portion of DRAM inside HDD is used for cache. Read cache and write cache commonly share the same space, so that part of write cache segments may be converted into read cache segments when necessary. However, some HDDs may have dedicated read or write cache for different purposes. In Chapter 4, I will show more details.

Conventional magnetic recording (CMR) is a relative concept. The longitudinal magnetic recording (LMR) HDD was a conventional concept to perpendicular magnetic recording (PMR) HDD in early 2000s. Nowadays, PMR is the dominant structure and is still in evolution. For example, SMR (shingled magnetic recording) is a new type of PMR already available in the market, while HAMR (heat-assistant magnetic recording) and MAMR (microwave-assistant magnetic recording) are emerging.

SMR HDD

SMR is the emergent technique being deployed to increase areal density in HDDs without drastic changes to the HDD mechanics [4, 5, 6, 7, 8]. Due to its shingled nature, SMR tends to favor large sequential writes over random ones. In this background section, I will give a general introduction to SMR characteristics.

The most significant feature of a SMR drive is its sequential write properties due to the shingled tracks. As shown in Figure 1-3, all physical sectors are written sequentially in a particular direction radially and are only rewritten after a wrap-around. Rewriting a previously written LBA will cause the previous write to be marked invalid and the LBA will be written to the next sequential physical sector.

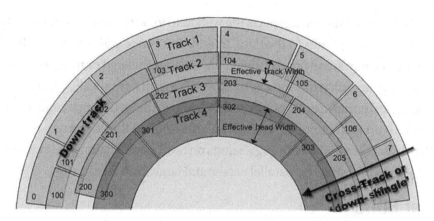

Figure 1-3. *Schematic of SMR*

Due to this log-structure-like sequential write feature (which is beneficial for write performance), the conventional LBA-to-PBA mapping (direct/static mapping) may not work well since any change in a block results in a read-modify-write access to all its consecutive blocks in the same zone, which can cause performance penalties. Therefore, indirect/dynamic mapping is usually applied. When an update happens, instead of an in-place rewrite, an out-of-place "new" write will be carried out, which leads to write implications; in other words, the data in the previous place becomes garbage and the new write claims additional space. In order to reuse those garbage blocks, a garbage collection (GC) procedure must be implemented.

Another concern of the out-of-place update is the potential harm to the sequential read performance. If some LBA-continuous requests are written into several different physical zones, the later LBA-continuous read request in the same LBA range cannot gain the actual benefit of the "logically sequential" read. The corresponding data management scheme can be implemented in three levels: drive, middleware, or host side. Although a few academic works have introduced in-place updates via a special data layout design, the out-of-place policy remains the main approach.

In general, a SMR drive expects the workload to be read/write sequentially, with infrequent updates to the data. In addition, since garbage data will generally occur at some points (unless data is never deleted or modified), idle time should be sufficiently long as to allow GC to run periodically without impacting external/user IO performance. Hence, the write-once-read-many (WORM) workload (archival) is a natural extension to the characteristics of SMR drives. Few other recent suggestions on SMR optimizations are available in [9], e.g., hybrid strategy, parallel access and large form factor.

Other HDDs

The PMR technique reached its theoretical limitation of areal density for conventional design ($1TB/in^2$) in recent years. The limiting factor is the onset of the super-paramagnetic limit as researchers strive towards smaller grained recording media. This levies a tradeoff between the signal-to-noise ratio (SNR) and the thermal stability of small grain media and the writability of a narrow track head, which restricts the ability to continue to scale CMR technology to higher areal densities [10].

Several promising technology alternatives have been explored to increase the areal density beyond the limit, such as two-dimensional magnetic recording (TDMR), heat-assisted magnetic recording, microwave-assisted magnetic recording [10], and bit-patterned magnetic recording (BPMR). Table 1-1 provides a brief category and Figure 1-5 shows the trends of these techniques.

Table 1-1. *New Techniques to Increase Areal Density*

Approaches	Reduce grain size and make grains harder to switch	Reduce bit width and/or length	Increase areal density/size, add heads and disks
Solutions	HAMR, MARM	SMR, HAMR, T-DMR	Helium drive, advanced mechanical designs, form factor optimization

In BPMR technology, each recording bit is stored in a fabricated magnetic island of around 10 nm. It has been proposed as a means for extending the super-paramagnetic limit of current granular media as illustrated in Figure 1-4 (a). The recording physics in BPMR are fundamentally different from conventional PMR, as the write and read scheme must be totally reestablished. A major shortcoming is the write synchronization requirement in which the write field must be timed to coincide with the locations of patterned islands. The total switching field distribution in the writing process, including various interference fields, must be less than the product of the bit length and the head field gradient to attain a high areal density up to 5 TB/in² theoretically.

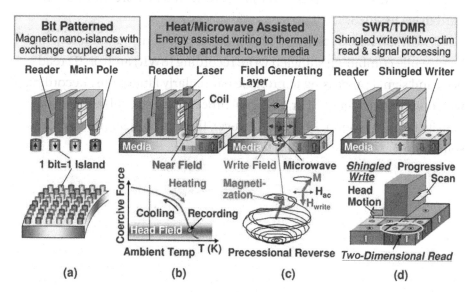

Figure 1-4. *Future options of HDD[10]*

HAMR and MAMR are two implementations of energy-assisted magnetic recording (EAMR). HAMR is proposed to overcome head writability issues. The core components of proposed HARM and MAMR technologies are a laser and a spin torque-driven microwave oscillator, respectively. In HAMR, the media have to be stable at much smaller grain sizes yet be writable at suitably elevated temperatures. The integration of HAMR and BPMR enables an extension of both technologies, with projected areal density up to about 100 Tb/in^2 based on the thermal stability of known magnetic materials [10]. Both WDC and Seagate announced their roadmap for EAMR. Seagate claimed that its HAMR-based HDDs will be due in late 2018,[2] while WDC declared that its MAMR will store 40TB on a hard drive by 2025.[3]

TDMR still uses a relatively conventional perpendicular medium and head, while combining shingled write recording (SWR) and/or 2D read back and signal processing to promise particularly large gains. Recording with energy assist on BPM or 2D signal processing will enable the areal density beyond around 5 Tb/in^2. However, there is no clear problem-free solution so far.

---

[2]www.anandtech.com/show/11315/seagate-ships-35th-millionth-smr-hdd-confirms-hamrbased-hard-drives-in-late-2018

[3]www.wdc.com/about-wd/newsroom/press-room/2017-10-11-western-digital-unveils-next-generation-technology-to-preserve-and-access-the-next-decade-of-big-data.html

Note that for HAMR/MAMR HDDs, the sequential access properties may be similar to SMR/TDMR. As the heater start-up/cool-down requires time, sequential access to reduce the status change is preferred.

One of other recent techniques to increase single device's capacity is the volumetric density scaling, such as adding more disc platters into one Helium-filled drive (less turbulence, thinner disks, and higher capacity) and designing a large form factor enclosure [9]. To further increase the capacity of single drives, some interesting designs have been suggested. For example, the dual-spindle design can access two disk clusters with two arms [11]. In this direction, more arms and disks are also possible, such as six arms and six disk spindles. Magnetic disk libraries and cartridge designs make the disk media exchangeable, similar to optical disks.

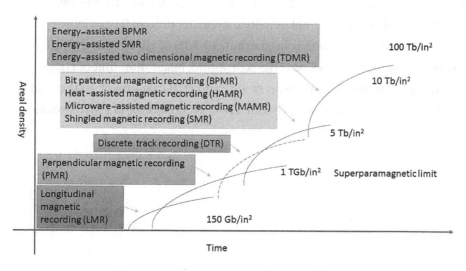

Figure 1-5. *Predicated density of future techniques[10]*

SSD

A solid-state drive/disk (SSD) is a solid-state storage device to store data persistently that utilizes integrated circuit assemblies as memory [12]. Electronic interfaces compatible with traditional HDDs, such as SAS and SATA, are primarily used in SSD technology. Recently, PCIe, SATA express, and M.2 have become more popular due to increased bandwidth requirements.

The internal memory chip of a SSD can be NOR-flash, NAND-flash, or some other emerging NVM (non-volatile memory). Most SSDs have started to use 3D TLC (tri-layer ceil) NAND-based flash memory as of 2017.

SSD is changing the storage industry. While the maximum areal storage density for HDDs is only 1.5 Tbit/in, the maximum for flash memory used in SSDs is 2.8 Tbit/in in laboratory demonstrations as of 2016. And SSD's overall areal density increasing ratio of flash memory is over 40% per year, which is larger than 10-20% of HDD. And the price decreasing ratio of SSD ($ per GB) is dropping faster than that of HDD.

Table 1-2 gives a comparison of SSD and HDD, where the SSD mainly refers to NAND-based devices, while HDD is conventional PMR devices.[4]

---

[4]Revised source from wiki and latest industry updates.

Table 1-2. *Comparison of HDD and SSD*

Attribute	SSD	HDD
Start-up time	Almost no delay because there is no requirement to prepare mechanical components (some μs to ms). Usually a few ms to switch from an automatic power-saving mode.	Up to several seconds for disk spin-up. Up to few hundred million seconds to wake up from idle mode.
Random access time	Typically less than 0.1 ms. Not a big performance bottleneck usually.	Typically from 2.5 (high-end server/enterprise drives) to 12 ms (laptop/mobile drives) mainly owing to seek time and rotational latency.
Read latency time	Usually low due to the direct data access from any location. For applications constrained by the HDD's positioning time, SSD has no issue in faster boot and application launch times (see Amdahl's Law). A clean Windows OS may spend less than 6 seconds to boot up.	Generally much larger than SSDs. The time is different for each seek due to different data locations on the media and the current read head position.[5] A clean Windows OS may spend more than 1 minute to boot up.

(*continued*)

---

[5]Usually, it ranges from 0 (sequential), ~ 0.5ms (1 track), ~ 0.2ms (head switch) to 10+ ms (long seek).

Table 1-2. (*continued*)

Attribute	SSD	HDD
Data transfer rate	Relatively consistent IO speed for relatively sequential IO. Performance is reduced when the portion of random smaller blocks is large. Typical value ranges from around 300MB/s to 2500MB/s for consumer products (commonly speed around 500MB/s at 2017). Up to multi-gigabyte per second for enterprise class.	Heavily depends on RPM, which usually ranges from 3,600 to 15,000 (although 20,000 RPM also exists). Typical transfer speed at about 200 MBps for 3.5-inch drive at 7200 RPM. Some high-end drives can be faster, up to 300 MBps. TPI and SPT are also influential factors.
Read performance	Generally independent on the data location in SSD. In few cases, sequential access may be affected by fragmentation.	Random seek is expensive. Fragmented files lead to the location of the data in different areas of the platter; therefore, response times are increased by multiple seeks of fragments.
Write performance	Write amplification may occur.[6] Wear leveling techniques are implemented to get this effect. However, the drive may unavoidably degrade at an observable rate due to SSD's nature.	CMR has no issue with write amplification. However, SMR may have an issue due to the out-of-place-update. GC is also required.

(continued)

---

[6]A performance degradation phenomenon where the NAND cells display a measurable drop in performance and may continue degrading throughout the SSD life cycle.

Table 1-2. (*continued*)

Attribute	SSD	HDD
Impacts of file system fragmentation	Relatively limited benefit to reading data sequentially, making fragmentation not significant for SSDs. Defragmentation would cause wear with additional writes.[7]	Many file systems get fragmented over time if frequently updated. Optimum performance maintenance requires periodic defragmentation, although this may not be a problem for modern file systems due to node design and background garbage collection.
Noise (acoustic) and vibration	SSDs are basically silent without moving parts. Sometimes, the high voltage generator (for erasing blocks) may produce pitch noise. Generally insensitive to vibration.	The moving parts (e.g., heads, actuator, and spindle motor) make characteristic sounds of whirring and clicking. Noise levels differ widely among models, and may be large.[8] Mobile disks are relatively quiet due to better mechanical design. Generally sensitive to vibration.[9]

(*continued*)

---

[7]A practical limit on the number of fragmentation exists in a file system for sustainment. In fact, subsequent file allocations may fail once that limit is reached. Therefore, defragmentation may still be needed to a lesser degree.

[8]Normally, the noise is high when the disk starts to spin up. The noise level of HDD is generally much lower than that of the cooling fans.

[9]When moving HDDs from a warm condition to a cold condition before operating it (or vise verse), a certain amount of acclimation time is required. Otherwise, internal condensation may occur and immediate operation may lead to damage of its internal components. In addition, the sudden atmospheric pressure change may also crash the head into the disc media.

Table 1-2. (*continued*)

Attribute	SSD	HDD
Data tiering	Hot data may move from slow devices to fast devices. It usually works with HDDs, although in some implementations, fast and slow SSDs are mixed.	HDDs are usually used as a slow tier in a hybrid system. Some striped disk arrays may provide comparable sequential access performance to SSDs.
Weight and size	Essentially small and lightweight due to the internal structure. They usually have the same form factors (e.g., 2.5-inch) as HDDs, but thinner, with plastic enclosures. The M.2 (Next Generation Form Factor) format makes them even smaller.	HDDs are usually heavier than SSDs, since their enclosures are made of metal in general. 2.5-inch drives typically weigh around 200 grams while 3.5-inch drives weigh over 600 grams (depending on the enclosure materials, motors, disc magnets/number, etc.). Some slim designs for mobile could be less than 6mm thin.

(*continued*)

Table 1-2. (*continued*)

Attribute	SSD	HDD
Reliability and lifetime	NO mechanical failure. However, the limited number of write cycles for each block may lead to data loss.[10] A controller failure can lead to an unusable SSD. Reliability differs quite considerably depending on different manufacturers, procedures, and models.[11]	Potential mechanical failures from the resulting wear and tear. The storage medium itself (magnetic platter) does not essentially degrade from R/W accesses.[12]
Cost per capacity[13]	Consumer-class SSD's NAND chip pricing has dropped rapidly: US$0.60 per GB in April, 2013, US$0.45, $0.37 and $0.24 per GB in April 2014, February 2015, and September 2016, respectively. The speed has slowed down since late 2016. Prices may change after 3D NAND becomes common.[14]	Consumer HDDs cost about US$0.032 and $0.042 per GB for 3.5-inch and 2.5-inch drives in May 2017. The price for enterprise HDDs is generally more than 1.5 times over that for consumers. Relatively stable prices in 2017 may be broken after MAMR/HAMR release.

(*continued*)

---

[10]A non-common SSD, which is based on DRAM, does not have a wearing issue.

[11]Leading SSDs have lower return rates than mechanical drives as of 2011, although some bad design and manufacturing results in return rates reaching 40% for specific drives. Power outage is one of the main SSD failure types. A survey in December 2013 for SSDs showed that survive rate from multiple power outages is low.

[12]Carnegie Mellon University conducted a study for both consumer-and enterprise-class HDDs in 2007 and SSD in 2015 [13, 14]. HDDs' average failure rate is 6 years, with life expectancy at 9-11 years.

[13]https://pcpartpicker.com/trends/internal-hard-drive/

[14]https://pcpartpicker.com/trends/price/internal-hard-drive/

Table 1-2. (*continued*)

Attribute	SSD	HDD
Storage capacity	Sizes up to 60TB by Seagate were available as of 2016. 120 to 512GB models were more common and less expensive.	HDDs of up to 10TB and 12TB were available in 2015 and 2016, respectively.
Read/write performance symmetry	Write speeds of less costly SSDs are typically significantly lower than their read speeds. (usually ≤1/3). Similar read and write speeds are expected in high-end SSDs.	Most HDDs have slightly longer/worse seek time for writing than for reading due to the longer settle time.
Free block availability and TRIM command	Write performance is significantly influenced by the availability of free, programmable blocks. The TRIM command can reclaim the old data blocks no longer in use; however, fewer free blocks cause performance downgrade even with TRIM.	CMR HDDs do not gain benefits from TRIM because they are not affected by free blocks. However, SMR performance is also restricted by the available of free zones. TRIM is required for dirty zones sometimes.

(*continued*)

Table 1-2. (*continued*)

Attribute	SSD	HDD
Power consumption	High performance flash-based SSDs generally require 1/2 to 1/3 of the power of HDDs. Emerging technologies like PCM/RRAM are more energy-efficient.[15]	2.5-inch drives consume 2 to 5 watts typically, while some highest-performance 3.5-inch drives may use around 12 watts on average, and up to about 20 watts. Some special designs for green data centers send the disk to idle/sleep when necessary. 1.8- inch format lower-power HDDs may use as little as 0.35 watts in idle mode.[16]

In summary, here is a SWOT analysis for NAND SSD:

- Strength

  - A mature technology widely employed by industries

  - Large scale/density, applicable for 3D techniques

  - A single drain contact per device group is required compared with NOR.

  - Relatively cheaper than other emerging NVM types for dollar/GB

---

[15]High-performance DRAM-based SSDs generally require as much power as HDDs, and a power connection is always required even when the system is idle.

[16]Disk spin-up takes much more power than that a normal operation. For a system with many drives, like a RAID or EC configured structure, staggered spin-up is needed to limit the peak power overload.

- Weakness

  - Asymmetric performance (slower write than read)

  - Program/erase cycle (block-based, no write-in-place)

  - Data retention (retention gets worse as flash scales down)

  - Endurance (limited write cycle compared with HDD and other emerging NVMs) 100-1000 slower than DRAM

  - 10-1000 slower than PCM and FeRAM

  - Usually, the higher the capacity, the lower the performance.

- Opportunity

  - Scaling focused solely on density; density is higher than magnetic HDD in general.

  - Decreased cost, which will be comparable with HDD in the near future

  - 3D schemes exist despite of complexity

  - Durability is improved to a certain degree together with fine-tuned wearing leverage algorithms.

  - Replacement for HDD in data centers as a mainstream choice (in particular, an all-flash array), although hybrid infrastructures will remain for some years.

- Threat

    - The extra connections used in the NOR architecture provide some additional flexibility when compared to NAND configuration.

    - The active development of MRAM/ReRAM may shake NAND flash's dominate position.

The real question is the market share of the two technologies. It is important how you measure the market share. By money gets you a very different answer than by bit. In the money arena, SSDs will rapidly overtake HDDs spend in the very near future, while by bit, HDDs will still dominate for some years.

There are some other storage devices using flash memory. Flash thumb drives are similar to SSD but with much lower speed and they are commonly used for mobile applications. Kingston Digital released 1TB capacity drives with an USB 3.0 interface (data transfer speeds up to 240 MB/s read and 160 MB/s write) in early 2017 and 2TB drives (up to 300 MB/s read and 200 MB/s write) in late 2017, which is similar to HDD's speed.

Small form size memory cards are also widely used in electronic devices, such as smartphones, tablets, cameras, and so on. Some common formats include CompactFlash, Memory Stick, SD/MicroSD/MiniSD, and xD. SanDisk introduced up to 1TB size of Extreme Pro series SD products in September 2016 and MicroSD up to 400GB in August 2017.

Hybrid Disk

A hybrid drive is a logical or physical storage device that integrate a fast storage medium such as a NAND/NOR flash SSD into a slow medium such as a HDD [15]. The fast device in a hybrid drive can act either as a cache for the data stored on the HDD or as a tier peering to HDD. In generally, the purpose is to improve the overall performance by keeping copies of the most frequently used data (hot data) on the faster component. Back in the mid-2000s, some hard drive manufacturers like Samsung and Seagate theorized the performance boost via SSD inside HDD. In 2007, Samsung and Seagate introduced the first hybrid drives using the Seagate Momentus PSD and Samsung SpinPoint MH80 products.

There are generally two types of hybrid disks. One is of a dual-drive structure (the tiering structure) where the SSD is the fast tier and HDD is the slow tier. Usually, the OS will recognize the devices with two sub-storage devices. Western Digital's Black2 products introduced in 2013 and TarDisk's TarDisk Pear in late 2015 are two examples of dual-drive devices. The other is an integrated structure (solid-state hybrid drive, SSHD) where the SSD acts as cache [16]. Users or OSs may see one storage device only without specific operations.

The hybrid disk drive can operate in either self-optimized (self-learning) mode or host-optimized mode. In the self-optimized mode of operation, the SSHD works independently from the host OS, so device drives determine all actions related to data identification and migration between the HDD and SSD. This mode lets the drive appear and operate to a host system exactly like a traditional drive. A typical drive is Seagate's Mobile and Laptop SSHD. Host- optimized mode is also called host-hinted mode, so the host makes the decision for the data allocations in HDD and SSD via SATA interface (since SATA version 3.2). This mode usually requires software/driver support from the OSs. Microsoft started to support the host-hinted operations in Windows 8.1 (a patch for version 8 is available), while patches for the Linux kernel have been developed since October 2014. Western Digital's first generation of SSHDs is in this category.

The market of hybrid disk drives may be narrow due to some inherited limitations:

- The performance is heavily application/workload dependent usually. But the drive may not be smart enough to be constrained by its resource.

- Block level optimization is no better or worse than file/ object level optimization due to less information on the workload. Thus it is not recommended to optimize the workload in the drive level.

- It is not well suited for a data center infrastructure's general purpose due to relatively static configurations of hybrid disks.

For the write path, some hold-up capacitors are used to simulate SCM (see the "Storage Devices" section of this chapter) with DRAM in some high-end SSDs. This essentially solves the write back problem. For the read path, customers generally prefer to manage different speed tiers of storage by themselves. They are very concerned with the access latency variance, and hybrid systems are very poor in this area. There is virtually no uptake of infrastructure-managed hybrid storage in Hyperscale or public cloud infrastructure. There are lots of deployments of hybrid structures. It is just managed at higher layers, not in the infrastructure itself. Table 1-3 provides more details.

Table 1-3. Comparison of Some NVMs

	STT-MRAM	PCMS 3D Xpoint	ReRAM	Flash NAND
Read latency	< 10ns	< 100ns	< 10ns	10–100us
Write latency	5ns	> 150ns	50ns	> 100us
Power consumption	Medium	Medium	Medium	High
Price (2016)	200–3000/Gb	$\leq$ 0.5/Gb	100/Gb	$\leq$ 0.05/Gb
Endurance(Nb cycles)	10^{12} to unlimited	10^8–10^9	10^5–10^{10}	10^5–10^6

Tape and Disc

Magnetic tape was first used to record computer data in 1951. It usually works with some specific tape drives only. Despite its slow speed, it is still widely used for cold data archiving. IBM and FujiFilm demonstrated a prototype BaFe Tape with 123 Gb/in^2 areal density and 220TB cartridge capacity in 2015. Sony and IBM further increased this number to 201 Gb/in^2 and 330TB into a tiny tape cartridge in 2017.[17] Instead of magnetic materials painted on the surface of conventional tape, Sony used a "sputtering" method to coat the tape with a multilayer magnetic metal film, which is thinner with narrower grains using vertical bits. Note that tape and HDD share many similarities in the servo control, such as servo pattern and nanometer precision.

An optical disc is a flat, usually circular disc that encodes binary data (bits) in the form of pits. An early optical disc system can be traced back to 1935. Since then, there have been four generations (a CD of about 700MB in the first generation, a DVD of about 4.7GB in the second generation, a standard Blu-ray disc of about 25GB in the third generation, and a fourth generation disc with more than 1TB data).

Both magnetic tapes and optical discs are usually accessed sequentially only. Some recent developments use robot arms make the change of tape/disc automatically. It is expected that tape and optical disc may still be active in the market for some years. In particular, due to much lower price per GB than other media, the tape seems to have a large potential market for extremely cold storage.

---

[17]https://arstechnica.com/information-technology/2017/08/ ibm-and-sony-cram-up-to-330tb-into-tiny-tape-cartridge/

Emerging NVMs

There are also many types of emerging NVMs on the way to mature or under an early stage of development [17, 10]:

- Phase-change memory (PCM), such as 3D X-point

- Magnetoresistive RAM (MRAM), such as STTRAM and Racetrack memory

- Resistive RAM (RRAM/ReRAM), such as Memristor, Conductive-bridging RAM (CBRAM), Oxy-ReRAM

- Ferroelectric RAM (FeRAM), such as FeFET

- Others, such as conductive metal oxide (CMOx), solid electrolyte, NRAM (nano RAM), ZRAM (zero-capacitor), quantum dot RAM, carbon nanotubes, polymer printed memory, etc.

STT-MRAM [18] (spin-transfer torque MRAM), using electron spin-induced change in magnetic moment, can replace low-density SRAM and DRAM, particularly for mobile and storage devices. Phase-change memory (PCM), making thermally induced physical phase changes between amorphous and crystalline states, has the ability to achieve a number of distinct intermediary states, thereby having the ability to hold multiple bits in a single cell. PCMS 3D Xpoint, announced by Intel and Micron in 2015, is based on changes in the resistance of the bulk material faster and is more stable than traditional PCM materials. ReRAM/CBRAM (conductive-bridging RAM) uses a metallic filament formation in electrolyte to storage, and FeRAM uses a ferroelectric layer instead of a dielectric layer to achieve nonvolatility [1]. Table 1-3 shows a simple comparison of them with NAND. A few of them could be in mass production within the next few years [19], although it might be still early to confirm which NVM technique is a winner in the competition, as they have their advantages and disadvantages. For example, let's use PCM as an example for its SWOT analysis.

- Strength

  - Relatively mature (large-scale demos and products) compared with other emerging NVMs

  - Industry consensus on materials, like GeSbTe or GST

  - Large resistance contrast, which leads to analog states for MLC

  - Much longer endurance than NAND Flash

  - High scalability (still works at ultra-small F) and back-end-of-the-line compatibility

  - Potential very high speed (depending on material and doping)

- Weakness

  - RESET step to high resistance requires melting – > power-hungry and thermal crosstalk?

  - To keep switching power down – > sub-lithographic feature and high-current access device

  - To fill a small feature – > atomic layer deposition or chemical vapor deposition techniques – > difficult now to replace GST with a better material

  - MLC strongly impacted by relaxation of amorphous phase – > resistance drift

  - 10-year retention at elevated temperatures (resistance drafts with time) can be an issue – > recrystallization

- Device characteristics change over time due to elemental segregation – > device failure

- Variability in small features broadens resistance distributions

- Opportunity

  - An order of magnitude lead over FeRAM, MRAM, etc.

  - NOR-replacement products now shipping – > if yield-learning successful and MLC (3-4 bits per cell successfully implemented in PCM technologies despite R-drift phenomenon in 2016)

  - Good for embedded NVM for SoC, Neuromorphic

  - Drift-mitigation and/or 3D access devices can offer high-density (i.e., low-cost), which means the opportunity for NAND replacement. Finally S-type, and then M-type SCM may follow.

  - Projected to reach 1.5B USD with an impressive CAGR of almost 84% by 2021

- Threat

  - Attained speed in practice is much slower than the theoretical speed; slow NOR-like interfaces

  - The current PCM SSD is only several times faster than SLC SSD, which is far away from the projection.

  - DRAM/SRAM replacement may be challenging due to fundamental endurance limitation.

  - PCM as a DRAM segment accounted for the major shares and dominated the market during 2016, which means a long way for S-SCM.

- A key challenge is to reduce reset (write) current; contact dimension scaling will help, but will slow progress.

- Engineering process

NAND techniques are also under active development, in particular, the 3D NAND. Compared with these emerging NVMs, NAND is relatively mature, dense, and cheap. However, it could be much slower than PCM and ReRAM. Meanwhile, its durance may be significantly lower than PCM, MRAM, and FeRAM in general.

Based on these NVMs, a special category called SCM (storage class memory) is introduced to fill the IO gap between SSD and DRAM (although it was initially for the gap between HDD and DRAM from IBM). It is further divided into storage-type SCM and memory-type SCM, depending on whether their speed is in magnitudes of microseconds or nanoseconds. Improved flash with 3D techniques, PCM, MRAM, RRAM, and FeRAM are some major techniques applied to SCM. This wide deployment of SCM to the computer/network systems and IoT systems will reshape the current architectures. In the very near future, we can see the impact of SCM to in-memory computing (e.g., application in cognitive computing), hyper-converge infrastructure, hybrid storage/cloud infrastructure (with remote direct memory access), etc. A brief outlook of these NVMs is illustrated in Figure 1-6, which is modified from the IBM's prediction.[18] In fact, the commercial version of Optane P4800X using 3D PCM-like techniques by Intel released in Nov 2017 has 750GB in capacity, 550K in IOPS, and 2.4/2.0 GB/ps in R/W throughput, while Z-NAND, a variant of 3D NAND by Samsung released in Jan 2018, has 800GB in capacity, 750K/150K in R/W IOPS, and 3.2 GB/ps in throughput.

---

[18]IBM Almaden Research Center, Storage Class Memory, Towards a disruptively low-cost solid-state non-volatile memory, 2013

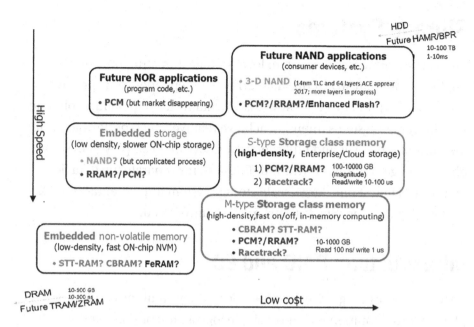

Figure 1-6. *Competitive outlook among emerging NVMs*

According to Yole Development's recent estimation,[19] the emerging NVM market will reach USD 4.6 billion by 2021, exhibiting an impressive growth of +110% per year, although the market size in 2015 was USD 53 million only. SCM will be the clear go-to market for emerging NVM in 2021. Marketsandmarkets[20] also predicts that the global non-volatile memory market is expected to reach USD 82.03 billion by 2022, at a CAGR of 9.50% between 2017 and 2022.

---

[19]www.yole.fr/

[20]www.marketsandmarkets.com/Market-Reports/non-volatile-memory-market-1371262.html

Storage Systems

This section discusses the system level storage infrastructure and implementation. RAID (redundant array of independent/inexpensive disks) and EC (erasure code) systems are mainly used for failure tolerance. Hybrid storage systems intend to achieve relatively high performance at low cost. Microserver and Ethernet drives have been employed in some object storage systems. Software-define systems separate the data flow and control flow. Some large-scale storage system implementations, like Hadoop/Spark, OpenStack, Ceph, are also introduced.

Infrastructure: RAID and EC

RAID as a data storage virtualization technology combines multiple physical drive components into a single logical unit or pool for the purposes of data redundancy, performance improvement, or both [20]. The Storage Networking Industry Association (SNIA) standardized RAID levels and their associated data formats from RAID 0 to RAID 6: "RAID 0 consists of striping, without mirroring or parity. RAID 1 consists of data mirroring, without parity or striping. RAID 2 consists of bit-level striping with dedicated Hammingcode parity. RAID 3 consists of byte-level striping with dedicated parity. RAID 4 consists of block-level striping with dedicated parity. RAID 5 consists of block-level striping with distributed parity. RAID 6 consists of block-level striping with double distributed parity." RAID 2-4 are generally not for practical usage. RAID levels can be nested, as in hybrid RAID. For example, RAID 10 and 50, which is RAID 1 and 5 based on RAID 0.

RAID can be implemented by either hardware or software. Hardware RAID controllers are expensive and proprietary, and usually used in enterprise environments. Software-based implementations have gained more popularity recently. Some RAID software is provided by modern

OSs and file systems, such as Linux, ZFS, GPFS, and Btrfs. Hardware-assisted RAID software implements RAID mechanisms in a standard drive controller chip with embedded proprietary firmware and drivers.

Nowadays, RAID systems are widely used in SMEs. Even in some data centers, RAID is still used as a fundamental structure for data protection. However, RAID is limited by its data reliability level, so only up to two disk failures can be tolerated by RAID 6, which is not secure enough for some critical applications. Thus, the erasure coding scheme emerged as an alternative to RAID. In EC, data is broken into fragments that are expanded and encoded with a configurable number of redundant pieces and are stored across different locations, such as disks, storage nodes, or geographical locations. Theoretically, EC can tolerate any number of disk failures, although up to four are used in a group practically. EC may also encounter some performance issues, particularly when the system is operated in downgraded or recovery mode.

Hybrid Systems

Although all-flash arrays are gaining in popularity, hybrid structures remain the mainstream in data centers, due to the trade-offs between cost, reliability, and performance. In early days, the hybrid storage system contained a HDD as the fast tier and tape as the backup tier [21] [22]. Later, fast access speed HDDs (such as 15kRPM and 10kRPM) acted as the performance tier, and slow speed HDDs (such as 7200RPM and 5400RPM) acted as the capacity tier [23]. With the development of non-volatile memory (NVM) technologies, such as NAND Flash [24], PCM [25], STTMRAM [18], and RRAM [19], the performance cost ratio of NVMs is increasing. Table 1-3 lists the performance and price comparison of some well-known NVMs. These NVMs with fast accessing speed can be used as the performance tier [17] [26] or cache [27] [28] [29] [30] in a modern hybrid system. Nowadays, SSD is the first choice of performance tier, and the high capacity shingled magnetic recording (SMR) drive is used often as the back-up tier [31].

When designing a hybrid storage system, the algorithms for the tier and cache storage architectures are slightly different, although the general framework is similar (see Figure 1-7). Fundamentally, tier storage architecture moves data to the fast storage area instead of copying the data in the cache storage architecture. But both have four important steps to accomplish. Firstly, data allocation policies are needed to control the data flow between different devices. Secondly, there should be an efficient address mapping mechanism between the SSD cache address and the main storage address. Thirdly, due to the size limitation of SSD cache compared with main storage HDDs, only the frequently and recently accessed data, which is called hot data, can be stored in the SSD cache/tier to improve the system efficiency. Therefore, a suitable hot data identification algorithm should be applied to identify the hot/cold data. When the hot data is detected, the data needs to be promoted when necessary. Thus a data migration algorithm is needed to control the hot/cold data flow to improve the future access efficiency. Lastly, a caching scheduling algorithm is employed for queuing behaviors, such as the queue size, synchronization, execution sequence.

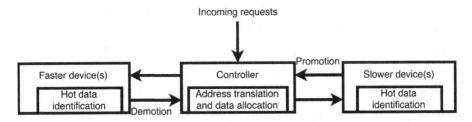

Figure 1-7. *General algorithms for hybrid storage system*

Data allocation: Data allocation is conducted by the host or device controller to allocate the incoming data to the most suitable storage location, such as hot data to SSD or cold data to HDD. Besides the properties of the data, the status of the devices is also considered during the allocation process, such as the queue length, capacity usage, bandwidth, etc.

Address mapping: Address mapping is required in a hybrid storage system because the capacities of the faster devices and slower devices are different. Due to the different address ranges, the accessing location of the incoming data needs to be translated to the actual address when the data is allocated to a different device. An address translation table is required to keep all these translation entries. If the address range is big, the memory consumption of the translation table is huge and the translation speed is reduced, which may affect the system performance.

Data migration (promotion/demotion): The data promotion is to migrate the data from the slower devices to the faster devices, and the data demotion is to migrate the data from the faster devices to the slower devices. This is called data migration. The data migration is usually conducted when the data in slower devices is identified as hot data or the data in faster devices is identified as cold data. In some research, the data migration is also done to balance the IOPS between the faster devices and slower devices.

Hot data identification: Hot data identification is important for the data migration to select the suitable data to promote and demote. It uses the properties of historical data to classify the incoming data as hot or cold. The classification is done by checking the accessing frequency and time of the data. Most frequently accessed and most recently accessed data are identified as hot data.

The hybrid storage architectures can be roughly classified into four categories, which are shown in Figure 1-8: (1) SSDs as a cache (caching method) of HDDs, (2) SSDs as a (high) tier (tiering method) to HDDs, (3) SSDs as the combination of tier and cache, and (4) HDDs with special purposes, such as HDDs utilized as the cache of SSDs. There are also some hybrid storage systems incorporating other types of NVMs into design consideration.

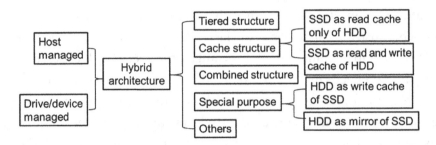

Figure 1-8. *The overall categories of the hybrid storage architectures*

Microservers and Ethernet Drives

A microserver is a server-class computer which is usually based on a system on a chip (SoC) architecture. The goal is to integrate most of the server motherboard functions onto a single microchip, except DRAM, boot FLASH, and power circuits. Ethernet Drive is one of its various forms.

In October 2013, Seagate Technology introduced its Kinetic Open Storage platform with claims that the technology would enable applications to talk directly to the storage device and eliminate the traditional storage server tier. The company shipped its first near-line Kinetic HDDs in late 2014. The Kinetic drive is described as a key-value server with dual Ethernet ports that support the basic put, get, and delete semantics of object storage, rather than read-write constructs of block storage. Clients access the drive through the Kinetic API that provides key-value access, third-party object access, and cluster, drive, and security management.

Introduced in May 2015, Toshiba's KVDrive uses the key-value API that Seagate open sourced rather than reinventing the wheel. Ceph or Gluster could run directly on Toshiba's KVDrive.

WDC/HGST's converged microserver based on its Open Ethernet architecture supports any Linux implementation. Theoretically, any network operating system can run directly in such a microserver.

Ceph and OpenStack Object Storage system have been demonstrated together with Red Had server. For example, in early 2016, WDC demonstrated a large scale Ceph distributed storage system with 504 drives and 4PB storage size.[21]

Software-Defined Storage

Software-defined storage is an emerging concept that is still in evolution. There are many different definitions from different organizations, such as the following:

- TechTarget:[22] SDS is an approach to data storage in which the programming that controls storage-related tasks is decoupled from the physical storage hardware (which places the emphasis on storage-related services rather than storage hardware).

- Webopedia:[23] SDS is storage infrastructure that is managed and automated by intelligent software as opposed to the storage hardware itself. In this way, the pooled storage infrastructure resources in a SDS environment (which can provide functionality such as deduplication, replication, thin provisioning, snapshots, and other backup and restore capabilities across a wide range of server hardware components) can be automatically and efficiently used to match the application needs of an enterprise.

---

[21]https://ceph.com/geen-categorie/500-osd-ceph-cluster/
[22]http://searchsdn.techtarget.com/definition/software-defined-storage
[23]www.webopedia.com/TERM/S/software-defined_storage_sds.html

- Wikipedia:[24] SDS is computer data storage software to manage policy-based provisioning and management of data storage independent of hardware. Software-defined storage definitions typically include a form of storage virtualization to separate the storage hardware from the software that manages the storage infrastructure. The software enabling a software-defined storage environment may also provide policy management for feature options such as deduplication, replication, thin provisioning, snapshots, and backup.

- Vmware:[25] SDS is the dynamic composition of storage services (such as snaps, clones, remote replication, deduplication, caching, tiering, encryption, archiving, compliance, searching, intelligent logics) aligned on application boundaries and driven by policy.

Despite of these different views, there are some common factors and features, which are summarized in Table 1-4 and Figure 1-9. Table 1-4 actually shows the three steps for SDS. First, the hardware should be decoupled from the software, such as the abstraction of logical storage services and capabilities from the underlying physical storage systems. Second, the storage resource is virtualized, such as pooling across multiple implementations. Third, automation mechanism is created with policy-driven storage provisioning with service-level agreements replacing technology details. Typical SDS products include GlusterFS, Ceph, and VMwareVirtual SAN. Figure 1-9 further gives the features in five aspects: data organization, scaling, persistent data store, storage service, and delivery model.

---

[24]https://en.wikipedia.org/wiki/Software-defined_storage
[25]www.vmware.com/files/pdf/solutions/VMware-Perspective-on-software-defined-storage-white-paper.pdf

Table 1-4. *Common Features of SDS*

Level	Steps	Consequence
Data plane, Control plane	Abstract (decouple/standardization, pooling/ virtualization), automation (policy-driven)	Faster, more efficient simpler

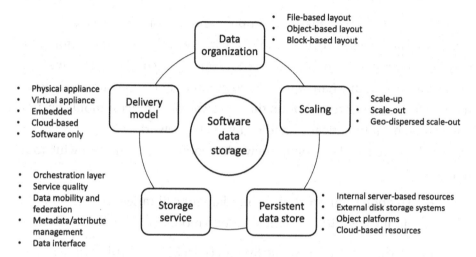

Figure 1-9. *The overall features of SDS*

SDS also leads to some other concepts, such as a software-defined data center (SDDC). Based on the report by IDC and IBM,[26] a SDDC is a loosely coupled set of software components that seek to virtualized and federate datacenter-wide hardware resources such as compute, storage, and network resources. The objective for a SDDC is to make the data center available in the form of an integrated service. Note that an implementation of SDS and SDDC may not be able to leave the support of another software defined concept, such as software-defined networking (SDN), which provides a fundamental change to the network infrastructure.

---

[26]www-05.ibm.com/de/events/solutionsconnect/pdfs/SolCon2013IBMDietmar NollTrendsimBereichStorage14062013.pdf

Implementation

I focus on some most recent software implementations for large scale systems with distributed storage components in this section.

Hadoop

Apache Hadoop,[27] an open-source implementation of MapReduce originating at Google, provides a software framework used for distributed storage and processing of big data sets. It consists of computer clusters built from commodity hardware. All the modules in Hadoop are designed under a fundamental assumption that hardware failures commonly occur and should be automatically handled by the framework.

The base Apache Hadoop framework is composed of the following four major modules:

- Hadoop Common has the fundamental libraries and utilities required by other Hadoop modules.

- Hadoop Distributed File System (HDFS) is a distributed file-system written in Java that stores data on commodity machines, providing very high aggregate bandwidth across the cluster.

- Hadoop YARN is a resource-management platform responsible for managing computing resources in clusters and using them for scheduling of users' applications.

- Hadoop MapReduce processes large scale data, as an implementation of the MapReduce programming model.

---

[27]http://Hadoop.apache.org/

38

HDFS stores large files (typically in the range of gigabytes to terabytes) across multiple machines. It achieves reliability by a replication mechanism, such as replicating the data across multiple hosts, and hence theoretically does not require RAID storage on hosts (some RAID configurations are still useful, like RAID 0). Data is stored on three nodes with the default replication value, 3. Data nodes can communicate with each other to rebalance data, to move copies around, and to keep the replication of data high. HDFS is not fully POSIX-compliant because the requirements for a POSIX file-system differ from the target goals for a Hadoop application. The trade-off of not-full compliance is increased performance for data throughput and support for non-POSIX operations such as Append. Although HDFS is the default distributed file system, it can be replaced by other file systems, such as FTP file systems, Ceph, Amazon S3, Windows Azure storage blobs (WASB), and others.

Nowadays, Hadoop is a large ecosystem with tens of different components. Figure 1-10[28] shows a simplified Hadoop ecosystem with an active expansion. In 2014, an in-memory data processing engine named Spark[29] was released to speed the MapReduce processing. These two projects share many common components.

---

[28]http://hadoopecosystemtable.github.io
[29]https://spark.apache.org/

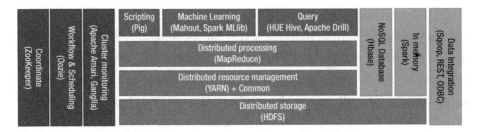

Figure 1-10. Hadoop ecosystem

OpenStack

OpenStack[30] is an open-source and free software platform for cloud computing, mostly deployed as an infrastructure-as-a-service (IaaS). It consists of interrelated components that control diverse, multi-vendor hardware pools of computing, storage, and networking resources throughout a data center. Therefore, the components can be basically divided into the categories of compute, storage, networking, and interface. For example, Nova is the cloud computing fabric controller as the main component of an IaaS system. Neutron is the component for managing networks and IP addresses. Figure 1-11 shows the overall architecture [32].

---

[30]www.openstack.org/

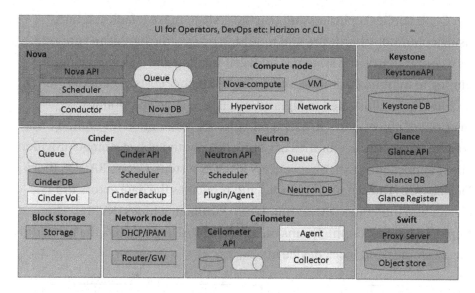

Figure 1-11. *Openstack architecture [32]*

OpenStack contains the block storage component called Cinder and an Object storage component called Swift. The Cinder system manages the creation, attaching, and detaching of the block devices to servers. Block storage volumes are fully integrated into Nova and the Horizon Dashboard, allowing cloud users to manage their own storage needs. Block storage is appropriate for performance-sensitive scenarios in both local server storage and storage platforms (e.g., Ceph, GlusterFS, GPFS, etc.). Swift is a scalable redundant storage system.

Ceph

Ceph,[31] an open-sourced and free distributed storage platform, provides a unified interfaces for object-, block-, and file-level storage [33, 34]. Ceph was initially created by Sage Weil for his doctoral dissertation. In 2012, Inktank Storage was founded by Weil for professional services and to support for Ceph.

---

[31]https://ceph.com

Ceph applies replicates and erasure code to make it fault-tolerant, using commodity hardware and requiring no specific hardware support. As a consequence, the system is both self-healing and self-managing, aiming to minimize administration time and other costs. A general architecture is illustrated in Figure 1-12. The reliable autonomic distributed object store (RADOS) provides the foundation for unified storage. The software libraries of Ceph's distributed object storage provide client applications with direct access RADOS system. Ceph's RADOS Block Device (RBD) automatically stripes and replicates the data across the cluster and integrates with kernel-based virtual machines (KVMs). The Ceph file system (CephFS) runs on top of LIBRADOS/RADOS that provides object storage and block device interfaces.

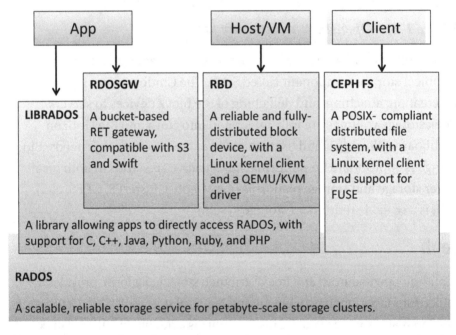

Figure 1-12. *Ceph architecture*

System Performance Evaluation

Many metrics are used to indicate the specification of storage devices or systems, in both static and dynamic sense. Table 1-5 gives a list of commonly used ones. When discussing performance, we usually refer to the dynamic specifications. In particular, IO performance is among the most important metrics.

Table 1-5. *Common Metrics for Storage Devices*

Metrics	Unit
Capacity	GB
Areal density (TPI, SPT)	GB/inch
Volumetric density	TB/liter
Write/read endurance	Times/years
Data retention time	Years
Speed (latency of IO access time; rand.)	Million seconds
Speed (bandwidth of IO access; seq.)	MB/second
Power consumption	Watts
Reliability (MTBF)	Hours
Power on/off transit time	Seconds
Shock and vibration	G-force
Temperature resistance	°C
Radiation resistance	Rad

Performance evaluation is an essential element of experimental computer science. It can be used to tune system parameters, to assess capacity requirements when assembling systems for production use, to compare the values of some different designs, and then provide guidance for the new development. As pointed out in [35], the three main factors that affect the performance of a computer system are

- The system's design

- The system's implementation

- The system's workload

These three factors influence and interact with each other. It is common for a system to perform well for one workload, but not for another. For a given storage system, its hardware design is usually fixed. However, it may provide some tuning parameters. If the parameters are also fixed in one scenario, the performance is usually "predictable" for a particular application. By running enough experiments, it is possible to obtain some patterns for the parameters related to the application's general workload properties. Then you may further tune the parameters. Sometimes, due to design limitations, the range of tuning parameters may be too narrow. Then you must redesign the system.

The most important three basic performance indexes are input/output operations per second (IOPS), throughput (TP), and response time (RT) [12].

- Throughput, also named bandwidth, is related to the data transfer rate and is the amount of data transferred to or from the storage devices within a time unit. Throughput is often measured in KB/sec, MB/sec, or GB/sec. For disk drives, it usually refers to the sequential access performance.

- IOPS means the IO operation transfer rate of the device or the number of transactions that can occur within a time unit. For disk drives, it usually refers to the random access performance.

- Response time, also named latency, is the time
  cost between a host command sent to the storage
  device and returned to the host, so it's the time cost
  of an IO request for the round trip. It is measured in
  milliseconds (ms) or microseconds (μs) and is often
  cited as an average (AVE) or maximum (MAX) response
  time. In a HDD specification, the average seek time and
  switch time are usually provided.

And the most important three access patterns are

- Block size, which is the data transfer length

- Read/write ratio, which is the mix of read and write
  operations

- Random/sequential ratio, which is the random or
  sequential nature of the data address requests

In addition, when considering consumer/client or enterprise devices/
systems, the focus may be different. For example, in some client use cases,
IOPS and bandwidth may be more critical than response time for HDD/
SSD devices, as long as the response times are not excessively slow, since the
typical client users would not usually notice a single IO taking a long time
(unless the OS or software application is waiting for a single specific response).
While client SSD use cases may mostly be interested in average response
times, the enterprise use cases are often more concerned with maximum
response times and the frequency and distribution of those times [12].

Performance vs. Workload

Workload can be categorized in several ways. From the domain point of
view, the workload can be imposed to the CPU, memory, bus, network,
etc. The level of details required in workload characterization relies on the
goal of the evaluation. It can be in the computer component level or in the

system application level. In the sense of applications, workload may be extracted from database, email, web service, desktop, etc.

An important difference among workload types is their rate [35], which makes the workload either static or dynamic. A static workload is one with a certain amount of work; when it is done, the job is completed. Usually, the job is several combinations of small sets of given applications. On the other hand, in a dynamic workload, work continues to arrive all the time; it is never done. It requires an identification of all possible jobs.

From practical point of view, the workload is divided into three categories: file-level, object-level, and block-level. In this book, I focus on block-level because most underlying storage devices are actually block devices, and the techniques applied to block-level analysis can be also used for file-level and object-level analysis.

Trace Collection and Analysis

Workload trace can be collected using both software and hardware tools, actively or passively. The inherited logging mechanism of some systems, which usually runs as background activates, is one of passive trace sources. Actively, you may require specific hardware (e.g., a data collection card, bus analyzer, etc.) and software (e.g., dtrace, iperf, blktrace, etc.) to collect traces purposely. These traces may be at different precision and detail levels. Sometimes you may also require the aid of benchmark tools when the environments of real applications are not available or inconvenient to obtain. Chapter 5 will discuss this in detail.

System Optimization

One of the main purposes of trace analysis is to identify the system performance bottleneck in various levels (e.g., component vs. system, user vs. kernel vs. hardware, etc.), and then optimize the overall system [36].

Take a simple IO stack as an example (Figure 1-13).[32] Access patterns generated by software applications must traverse the IO stack in order to get from the user space to the storage devices and back again. This movement indicates that the IOs will be impacted by the file system and various drivers as they pass them up or down the IO stack, such as coalescing small IO data transfers into a fewer larger IO data transfers, splitting large sequential IO data transfers into multiple concurrent random IO data transfers, and using the faster file system cache while deferring IO commits to the SSD.

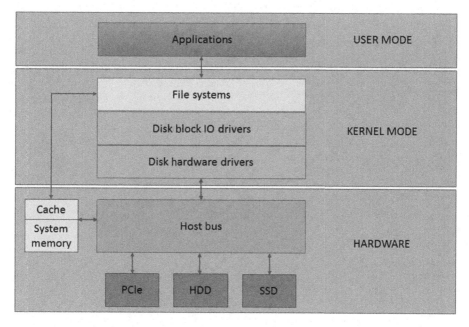

Figure 1-13. *IO stack*

In this book, I will provide some practical examples, ranging from single devices to complex systems, to show how the workload analysis can be applied to system optimization and design.

---

[32]A detailed Linux storage stack diagram can be found at www.thomas-krenn.com/en/wiki/Linux Storage Stack Diagram. The latest version, 4.10, was created at March 2017. [12]

CHAPTER 2

Trace Characteristics

Trace is usually classified as three levels: block level, file level, and object level. They share many common metrics, although each has its own unique properties. In this chapter, I will discuss block-level trace metrics in detail since the block-level trace provides more fundamental information on storage systems than other two levels. For simplicity of representation, I divide the metrics into two categories: the basic ones and the advanced ones. The meanings and performance impacts of these metrics are explained in detail.

Workload Properties

Workload can be collected and viewed in different abstract levels. Usually, there are three different levels, as show in Figure 2-1 [37]. The functional view indicates the users' behaviors, which aim to facilitate comparison between, say, a relational database system and a MapReduce system that serves the equivalent functional aims of some enterprise data warehouse management workload. It enables a large range of equivalent systems to be compared. It lacks tracing capabilities for large-scale, data-centric systems. The system view captures workload behavior at the highest level of abstraction that we can trace in large-scale data-centric systems currently. For example, this translates to the jobs steam and job characteristics in MapReduce. For enterprise network storage, this is the data accesses stream at the application, session, file, and directory levels. The physical view

© Jun Xu 2018
J. Xu, *Block Trace Analysis and Storage System Optimization*,
https://doi.org/10.1007/978-1-4842-3928-5_2

describes a workload in terms of hardware component behaviors, such as
the CPU, memory, disk, and network activities during workload execution.
It depends on hardware, software, or even configuration changes.

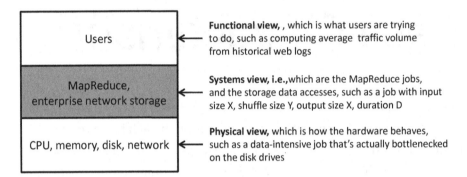

Figure 2-1. *Typical workload abstraction level*

The basic workload metrics are generally explicit and easily observed
directly or calculated with very simple formulations. Some examples are
listed in Table 2-1. However, the advanced ones are implicit and formulated
in relatively complex forms/rules. See Table 2-2 for few advanced metrics.
More details will be described in the next two sections of this chapter.

Table 2-1. *Examples of Basic Metrics*

Basic Metrics

Read to write ratio	Request size distribution	LBA range/ randomness	Inter-arrival time
The ratio between read and write operations in command number or total size	Request size, usually further count for total, read, and write	In a virtual volume, LBA can be used to represent the randomness in space. Otherwise, specify the device number.	Request arrival rate, idle time, busy time

With system-level information, queue depth, average response time, bus time, etc.
can be also included.

Table 2-2. *Examples of Advanced Metrics*

Advanced Metrics

Spatial locality	Temporal locality	Read/write dependency	Priority-related metrics
The small distance of two requests means that soon after referencing r_i you find a reference to the nearby address r_j.	The same address is referenced again after d steps. A concept closely related to temporal locality is popularity.	Three categories: true (read on write), output (write on write), and anti (write on read)	Request priority determines the execution sequence; it also includes the properties of synchronized vs. asynchronous.

In most cases, cache-related, cluster-related, and/or networked-related metrics should be included.

Note that the meaning of "block" in HDD and SSD is different. However, the definition of one sector as one block in HDD is used here. In addition, there are some different formats for sectors, such as 512, 512e, 4k, 4kn, etc. Without particular comments, assume that one sector is equal to 512 bytes for representation simplicity.

A block-level trace usually contains some common fields, like arrival time, completion time, LBA (first or last LBA), request size, operational mode (read or write, sync or async), etc. Some other fields, like bus time and merge time, depend on the trace collection tools. Table 2-3 gives an example of trace. For the ith request, r_i, denotes its arrival and completion action time as D_i and C_i. Usually, we arrange all N requests in sequence of D_i, *i.e.* $(r_1, \ldots, r_i, \ldots, r_n)$.

Table 2-3. *An Example of Block Trace*

Order	Arrival time (s)	Completion time (s)	First LBA	Size	Mode
1	0.026216	0.027506	902553856	1024	0
2	0.026790	0.027719	197306368	8	0
3	0.036680	0.039502	902554880	1024	0
4	0.039618	0.044770	197306368	16	1
5	0.039654	15.079936	197306368	16	1
6	0.044542	0.046394	902555904	1024	0
7	0.044865	0.046513	197306376	8	0
8	0.054996	0.055265	2657576	8	0
9	0.059638	0.059905	197306376	16	0
10	0.081950	0.083162	902556928	1024	0
11	0.089740	0.089960	197306384	8	1
12	0.092741	0.093955	902558976	1024	0
13	0.093261	0.095268	902557952	1024	0
14	0.112958	0.114461	902560000	1024	0
15	0.113097	0.115717	902561024	1024	0
16	0.114820	0.115926	197306384	8	0
17	0.135434	0.136744	902562048	1024	0
18	0.136436	0.136963	197306384	16	1
19	0.150173	0.151625	902563072	1024	0
20	0.150260	0.152809	902564096	1024	0

Basic Metrics

Basic metrics are usually simple and easy for observation. But this does not mean they contain less information than advanced metrics. In some cases, basic metrics are good enough to interpret the workload properties.

LBA Distribution

From the curve of LBA distribution vs. time, you can easily observe the randomness/sequence of IO access. Figure 2-2 gives two examples of the write-only requests' LBA distribution. The left plot shows a sequential access from LBA $6.7 * 10^8$ to $6.8 * 10^8$. The right plot mixes with sequential and random write accesses. Figure 2-3 shows that the IO pattern is combined with random read accesses and mixed write accesses. It's clear that write access is more sequential than read access, as the write access contains several sequential streams. Note that there may exist a small gap between two continuous requests sometimes, although it may look sequential visually from the plot. However, these near sequential IO patterns can be accessed sequentially in most cases.

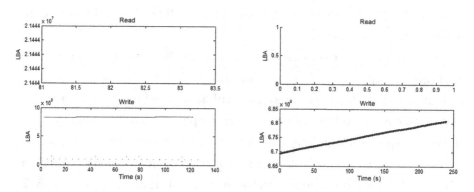

Figure 2-2. LBA distribution from a Ceph node

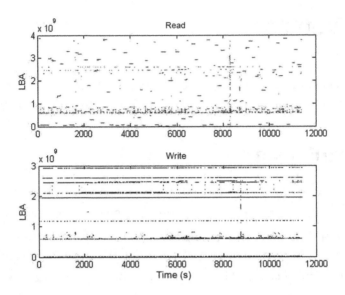

Figure 2-3. *LBA distribution from a Hadoop node*

Size Distribution

In general, the drive (whatever HDD or SSD) is in favor of sequential access, so the sequential access has much higher throughput than the random access, in particular for HDD. And the request size also matters especially when the disk queue is short, which will be clearly illustrated in Chapter 4 in Figures 4-2 and 4-3.

Figure 2-4 plots the request frequency and CDF (cumulative density function) vs. request size. For the distribution of write requests, you can see that the percentage of the requests with size 1024 blocks are almost 50% in this case, which usually means the IO pattern is dominated by large size requests. Note that due to OS/FS and disk drive limitation, the maximum request size is usually 1024 blocks, so even if the user requests a 1MB size file, it will be divided into two IO requests internally (assume 512 bytes per block).

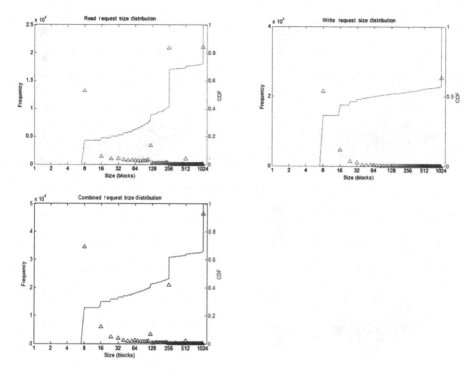

Figure 2-4. *Size distribution from a Hadoop node*

If you further need to know the size distribution with respect to (wrt) LBA range, you may have plots like Figure 2-5, from which you can learn more about the hot range with size information. Since you know that the transfer speed of different location in a HDD (e.g., ID vs. MD vs. OD) is different, the LBA can roughly tell the relative speed with the request size information.

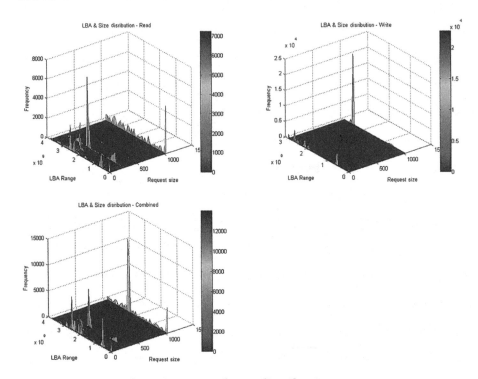

Figure 2-5. *Combined LBA and size distribution*

Read/Write Distribution

Read and write accesses may have different performance in drives. For HDD, the difference may be slight. However, for SSD, the gap could be large for the consumer class. In addition, read and write access may have dependencies on each other. For example, when a new write is just completed, the data may be still in the cache. An immediate read may access the data from the cache directly, instead of a media operation. Thus the visualization of distribution time can provide an intuitive view on the dependency. You can plot the data in a single figure or in two separate figures, as in Figure 2-3.

Table 2-4. Required Fields for Metrics Calculation

	Arrival time	Completion time	LBA	Request size	Mode operation
LBA distribution	Y (or)	Y (or)	Y		
Size distribution				Y	
IOPS	Y	Y (or)			
Throughput	Y	Y (or)		Y	
Queue length/depth	Y (or)	Y (or)			
Busy/idle time	Y	Y			
Read/write distribution	Y (or)	Y (or)			Y
Inter-arrival time distribution	Y				
Inter-completion time distribution		Y			

Inter-Arrival and Inter-Completion Time

Inter-arrival time is defined as the time interval between two sequentially arrived requests: $\delta t_i = D_i - D_{i-1}$. Similarity, inter-completion time is defined as $\delta \bar{t}_i = \bar{C}_i - \bar{C}_{i-1}$, where $\bar{C}_i$ is reordered C_i based on a completion time sequence. δt_i is a direct indictor of the workload burstiness [38], together with the supposed-to-be average completion time of requests. When the average δt_i is much smaller than $\delta \bar{t}_i$, it usually means the system is under a stressed workload, which may be beyond the storage device's capability. In a sense, these two indictors are closely related to IOPS.

IOPS and Throughput

IOPS is usually defined as the IO number Δn per unit time Δt seconds, such as $IOPS = \dfrac{\Delta n}{\Delta t}$. The unit time is preset by users, at perhpas 1 second. Similarly, throughput is the request size ΔS per unit time, so $TP = \dfrac{\Delta s}{\Delta t}$. Note that they are in a sense average values within a given unit time/time-window. For different Δt, IOPS and throughput may have different values. Usually, a larger Δt leads to a smoother curve. Figure 2-6 shows an example with data collected from a HDD node of a Ceph cluster. You can see that the IOPS ranges from 60 to 160 in the figure of Δt=1 second, while it is 80–120 when Δt=6 seconds. In particular, when the workload contains many bursts, the maximum and minimum IOPS values for different Δt may vary largely.

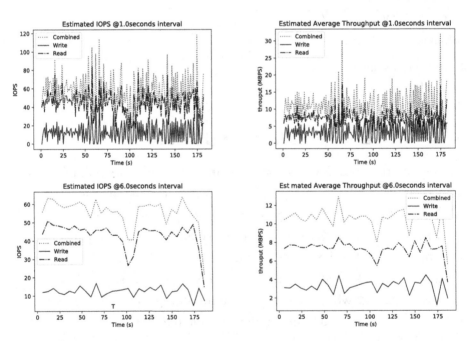

Figure 2-6. *Average IOPS and throughput with different time window*

The curves of the two metrics vs. time can be used to observe the workload burst visually. However, choose Δt carefully. A too-large Δt may smooth the curve but remove the IO burst. A practical choice is related to the average inter-arrival time, so Δt may be a few times the average inter-arrival time, but not too much.

Alternatively, you can fix Δn. For example, you may set Δn=20, and let Δt be various.

A complex setting is that you may let both Δt and Δn various. For example, let $\Delta n \leq 10$ and $\Delta t = 1$ second as the constraint. If within $\Delta t = 1$ second, there are Δn within the range, do the average. Otherwise, if $\Delta n > 10$, choose a time window that $\Delta n = 10$, and then do the average.

Another trivial issue when drawing the curve is the time, so the average value happens at the beginning, middle, or end of Δt. For example, if you choose the end of Δt, you may have the following formulations:

- $IO(t_j)$ = the total number of IOs based on the range calculated by D_i, so $IO(D_i)$, where D_i is within an interval $[t_{j-1} \, t_j]$

- $R(t_j)$ = the summation of request size of $IO(D_i)$

- Average IOPS at $t_j = IO(t_{j-1})/\Delta t$

- Average request size at $t_j = R(t_{j-1})/IO(t_{j-1})$

- Average throughput at $t_j = R(t_{j-1})/\Delta t$

You can also apply moving average techniques here; there is an overlap between two continuous "average" metrics.

Response Time

Response time is generally combined by the waiting (or queuing) time T_w and access (or service) time T_a, i.e., $T_{res} = T_a + T_w$. The service time is the time cost in service, such as disk access time. The queuing time is the cost when the request waits in the queue before it is sent for actual execution. When the trace is collected from the external bus (IO driver), such as SATA/SAS, the response time of r_i is calculated by $C_i - D_i$.

Queue Length/Depth

There are at least two queues in HDDs. One is along with the IO driver, which is influenced by the OS and FS, so the OS and/or FS may change the order of IOs to send to the disk drive based on some schedulers. The length is usually up to a trace collected externally only reflects the length in the IO driver. You can estimate the queue depth based on either arrival time or complete time of requests. They may have slightly differences. Let's denote one queue's D and C as D_i and C_i in sequence.

- IO driver queue depth just before command arrived (Q_{d1})

  - The queue depth just before D_i (instant queue depth $Q(D_i)$) = the number of requests whose C time >= D_i and D time < D_i

- IO driver queue depth just after command completed (Q_{d2})

  - The queue depth just after C_i (instant queue depth $Q(C_i)$) = the number of requests whose C time >= C_i and D time < C_i

- Average queue depth

  - Estimated average queue depth during non-idle period: $\sum_i((Q_{d1}+Q_{d2})/2 * (D_i - C_i))/\sum_i(D_i - C_i)$

  - Effective average queue depth in time interval: Sampling at Δt seconds

Figure 2-7 gives an illustration of Q_{d1} and Q_{d2}, where blue signs with arrows show the IO requests in time order. It also illustrates a few Q_{d1} and Q_{d2} for these requests. Table 2-5 further gives an example to show how the queue depth is calculated based on Q_{d1}. Figure 2-8 shows the estimated queue depth from a Hadoop node. It looks like the average queue depth is quite high, which means a high workload. However, zoom into the plot to check the intervals in-between the queues. In this example, the scale of the x-axis is 100 instead of 12000 to show more information.

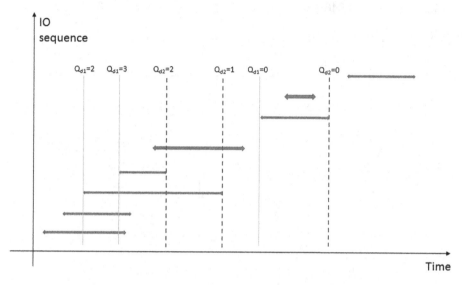

Figure 2-7. *Illustration of queue length*

Table 2-5. *Estimated queue depth and idle time*

Arrival time	Completion time	Queue depth	Idle time
0.00007	0.00036	0	-
0.01130	0.01157	0	1.09E–02
0.01134	0.01288	1	0
0.02622	0.02751	0	1.33E–02
0.02679	0.02772	1	0
0.03668	0.03950	0	8.96E–03
0.03962	0.04477	0	1.17E–04

(continued)

Table 2-5. (*continued*)

Arrival time	Completion time	Queue depth	Idle time
0.03965	15.07994	1	0
0.04454	0.04639	2	0
0.04486	0.04651	2	0
0.05500	0.05526	1	0

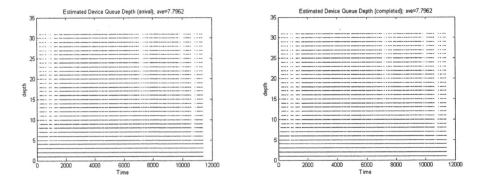

Figure 2-8. *Queue depth using arrival and completed time from a Hadoop node*

The other is the HDD internal queue for actual execution with mechanical parts. Some scheduling algorithms, such as SCAN and RPO (rotational positioning optimization), are applied here to attempt to minimize a given operation time. Vender special commands (VSCs) can be used to collect the internal queue information. RPO tries to minimize the summation of seek time and rotational latency of requests in the queue. Theoretically, a longer queue means the scheduler has more events to select, and the overall operational time can be reduced further (for a pure random access). However, in practice, when the queue length reaches a certain level, the performance does not increase, which is illustrated in Figures 4-2 and 4-3. Without VSC, we may only use the external IO queue status to approximate the internal queue status. This is reasonable in a sense because a HDD can only handle one request per time.[1] However, for SSD, the situation is much more complex due to parallel processing.

Busy/Idle Time

When a disk is under an IO operation (including both foreground and background activities), the disk is busy; otherwise, it is in idle mode. These two metrics are useful when you intend to design some background operations for disks, such as defragmentation, address remapping, sector scanning, etc. As some of these operations require over hundred milliseconds to complete, the estimated busy or idle time will be estimated to show whether the performance will be affected by background operations.

However, without VSC to extract the drive internal trace log, you may not get the busy/idle time directly. Thus we may only approximate the time from the external trace when the internal trace is unavailable. The basic idea is to compare the completion time of requests in the queue with the new requests' arrival time. If the completion time is later than the new arrival time, it means the drive is still busy at this arrival time. Otherwise, it is counted as idle time (although there may be some background activities inside disk drives; but you can assume that the user/external requests have higher priority than background activities). In other words, the calculation of idle time is heavily related to the queue depth, so only when queue depth is zerois there a chance to exist an idle interval.

Let's consider the trace in Table 2-3. The completion time 0.027506s of the first request is later than the arrival time of 0.026790s of the second request, so the disk is busy at 0.026790s. However, the completion time

---

[1]This may be not true for some modern disks with new architectures, such as MBC, SMR, and Egress, where write requests may be accessed in batch.

0.027719s of the second request is earlier than the arrival time 0.036680s of the third request, you may estimate that the drive have the idle time of 0.036680–0.027719=0.009s. Table 2-5 shows the result.

Figure 2-9 has the same data set as Figure 2-8. Although the queue depth is high in Figure 2-8, you can still observe many idle intervals for the disk.

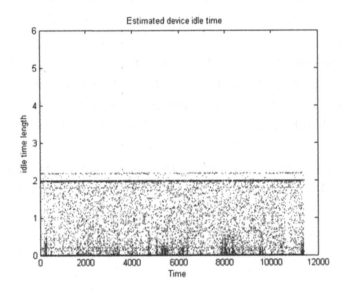

Figure 2-9. *Estimated idle time from a Hadoop node*

Advanced Metrics

The workload from the real world is usually complex. Even for those claimed as sequential workloads, such as a Hadoop HDFS write or Ceph Bluestore write, the actual IO pattern in the block level is mixed with sequence and randomness, as well as read and write. The advanced metrics attempt to provide insights into these traces.

Sequence vs. Randomness

The sequence and randomness of a workload are somehow subjective in some engineers' view, as it is not easy to clearly state whether a workload is more sequential or random when it is mixed. In addition, the "feeling" of sequence is also different in different cases. For example, some requests with very small gaps among them may be also considered as (near) sequential.

In my view, it may be quantified under different scenarios, such as the scheduler algorithm, queue length, etc. That means this property is objective when all the conditions are fixed. For example, consider a burst workload of write requests within a small LBA range. Some of the requests are actually continuous in LBA, although they do not arrive in order. If a FIFO scheduling policy is applied, this workload is random, as the disk has to seek to different locations for each request. When a simple SCAN or RPO scheduling algorithm is applied, the requests will be reordered and some will become sequential, if there is a long enough queue. Assume that there are N requests. So there are up to N–1 seeks (in a strict definition, a request is considered as a random one, if there is a seek in term of LBA). Let the random access number as N_r and sequential access as N_s, so you can obtain a ratio of randomness vs. sequence for a given workload under a fixed scenario.

Sequential and Near Sequential Streams

This metric directly indicates the sequence degree of the workload. In general, a command is sequential when it comes after a similar command whose requested block LBAs just prior to this new command. Hence, sequential reads follow read commands and sequential writes follow write commands; but there are some subtleties to this definition. *(Strictly) sequential stream* means that the current and previous commands are of the same type (r/w) and the new command's starting LBA immediately follows the previous one. *Near sequential stream* means that there must be an earlier command of the same type (read or write) whose LBA range comes before and near the start of this new command. For a sequential stream, multiple streams may interleave with each other. There are user settings to affect these subtleties, allowing us to describe the variations of sequential command situations.

Queued sequence stream: In a time-order request stream, some are adjacent to each other (possible within a time window), such that last LBA(r_i)+1 = first_LBA (r_j), where $i < j$, $D_j - D_i < \delta t$ and $\delta t > 0$ is an aging time.

In this way, $j \geq i + 1$ is possible because of interleaved sequence streams. However in practice, a command queue with queue length N is required to identify the sequence, instead of only checking the exactly adjacent requests wherein. Once a new request enters the queue, it searches the queue to check the sequence match. If a match is found, it's merged into the queue; otherwise, it adds a new entry to the queue. If the queue is full, it removes the entry using a replacement rule (e.g., FIFO or LRU).

Generally, the larger N, the larger number of sequence requests detected (M_2) in each stream, and the smaller number of sequence streams (M_1). The key is to find a large enough N such that the number of sequence streams detected is stable.

Queued sequence stream with constraint: In practice, a large block request S (e.g., $S \geq 1024$) is also counted as a sequential request. Hence an alternative method in considering the stream i is to determine the total size of a stream S_i together with M_2, so if $S_i \geq S$ and $M_2 \geq M$, then i is considered a sequence stream, where S and M are thresholds.

Queued near-sequence stream: Finally, it is possible that a small gap between LBA requests exists such that in a time-ordered request stream, some requests are near to each other within a time window. Once a new request is considered near-sequential to the previous one, the stream's last LBA is updated as the new request's last LBA (hole is filled for simplicity),

so last LBA(r_i) +1≤ first LBA(r_j) and last LBA(r_i) +δd ≥ first LBA(r_j),
where $i < j$ and 0<D_j–D_i< δt. δd > 0 is a small integer in blocks, such as 64.
A command queue is required to detect the interleaved streams and the size
constraints are also applicable to near-sequence streams. See Figure 2-10.

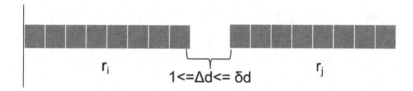

Figure 2-10. *An example of near sequence stream*

Let's look at an example in Table 2-6. Assume that these requests arrive
in a *t*-seconds time window. It is obvious that all requests are random by
comparing the last LBA of the pervious request and first LBA of the current
request in terms of FIFO. In this case, there are seven times of seeks and
N_r =8 and N_s =0. In this sense, the workload is random because there is
no sequential stream. However, if you reorder the requests with the aid of
queue in term of LBA, so the request order < 263158(7)4 >, you have N_r =3
and N_s =4, in terms of (strict) sequential streams. Note that the request
number 7 is absorbed by the request number 8 during the reordering. So
M_2=2 (< 2631 > and < 58(7) >) for (strictly) sequential stream. With two
constraints, S = 1024 and M_2 = 2, you have (< 58(7) > and < 4 >). The stream
of < 2631 > is removed due to small size.

When considering a near sequential stream with Δd=64 and 512,
you have M_2=3 (< 2631 > and < 58(7) > and < 4 >) and 1 (< 263158(7)4 >),
respectively, under strictly sequential stream.

Table 2-6. *An Example of LBA Sequence and Randomness*

Order	First LBA	Last LBA	Order	First LBA	Last LBA
1	128	135	5	256	511
2	0	7	6	8	63
3	64	127	7	640	647
4	1536	2047	8	512	1279

From this example, here are the following variables:

- N_{s1}: The number of requests with sequential access

- N_{s2}: The number of requests with near sequential access and LBA gap

- N_r: The number of the remaining requests

These variables have strong connection with the logical seek defined in the next section.

The practical gap size Δd in a real application is usually determined by the system performance tolerance. Usually, it is up to few track sizes. For example, if an acceptable tolerance is 5ms, then Δd can be up to 1536 blocks based on disk model of 10K RPM drive with track/head switch time at 1ms and average track size at 1.5MB. For random access, the average rotational latency is 3ms. Assume a 50% chance of the new request in the same track and 50% chance in next track (the actual probability is coupled with Δd). Then you have 5-(3+1)*50%=3ms for further rotation, which is about half a track size, so 1536 blocks.[2]

---

[2]This calculation is for a conventional HDD. For SMR or MBC drives, it may be different.

Sequential ratio: Due to the different views on the sequence, the definition of sequential ratio is also varied. Below, few examples are listed.

- DEF1: The summation of sequential commands detected with S and M_2 thresholds / total commands

- DEF2: (The summation of sequential commands detected with S and M_2 thresholds - total sequential streams) / total commands

- DEF3: The summation of the request size of sequential commands detected with S and M_2 thresholds / total request size of all commands

- DEF4: (The summation of the request size of sequential commands detected with S and M_2 thresholds - the summation of the size of the first command in sequential streams) / total request size of all commands

If you remove size constraint S, you get another four definitions.

Spatial Locality and Logical Seek Distance

Locality, as a special case of correlation of a variable with itself over short to medium ranges, can be visualized as a 2D probability surface $p(s, d)$, showing the probability that the first time an address s bytes away will be referenced in exactly d cycles. There are generally two types of locality: spatial locality and temporal locality. For spatial locality, if the distance $s = |x_i - x_j|$ is small, it implies that not long after referencing address x_i you will discover a reference to the adjacent address x_j. Temporal locality will be discussed in the next subsection.

Note that only LBAs are provided in most traces, not the physical block address (PBA). Because different HDDs may not have exactly same data layouts (such as serpentine), identical LBA layouts between different HDDs can result in different PBAs. However, the difference is usually very small if their data layout is similar. Therefore, analyzing logical distance is also meaningful.

Below I discuss two distances to indicate spatial and temporal localities, respectively [35].

Logical Seek Distance

This metric is an indicator for spatial locality. It defines the logical block/LBA distance between "consecutively" device-received IOs.

- Non-queued next: The simplest case, which calculate the distance between two exactly consecutive IOs.

- Non-queued closest: The absolute closest distance = min ($\|$last_LBA(r_{j-1})– first_LBA(r_j) $\|$, $\|$last_LBA(r_j) – first_LBA(r_{j+1})$\|$), where r_j is the current IO. The closest distance is the signed value of the absolute close distance, where $\| \cdot \|$ indicates the absolute value.

- Queued next: Simulates a queue with certain rules such that the absolute closest distance = min ($\|$last_LBA(r_i)– first_LBA(r_j)$\|$), i=1,. . . ,$n_i \leq N$, where $n_i \leq N$ is the current queue length, and r_i is the IO in the queue.

- Queued closest: Simulates a queue such that the absolute closest distance = min($\|$last_LBA(r_i) – first_LBA(r_j) $\|_{i=1,...,n_i}$, $\|$last_LBA(r_j) – first_LBA(r_j+1)$\|$).

In general, $\|$Queued closest $\| \leq \|$Non-queued closest $\| \leq \|$Non-queued next$\|$. For the distance, you can further define three values: mean, median, mode. Mode indicates the most frequent number such that the larger the counter for mode = 0, the better the sequence.

Temporal Locality and Logical Stack Distance

Temporal locality means that the same address is referenced again after d steps. Popularity is a terminus that is closely related to temporal locality.

Logical Stack Distance

If an LBA in r_i is referred to again after some time by another request r_j, the command distance between the two requests is defined as (simplified) the logical stack distance, an important temporal locality index. Let's take write requests as an example. If the distance is small enough (e.g., smaller than the HDD's DRAM cache queue size), it might be a hit in the DRAM cache; otherwise, a disk update is required for the write. If the frequency of the write for a certain range of distance is high, it means the update frequency is high.

Unlike the case in [35], we are more interested in queued stack distance with consideration of cache. Therefore, let's also look into read/write dependency. The details will be discussed in later in this chapter.

Burstiness and Self-Similarity

I/O requests almost never occur singly but tend to arrive in groups because, if there were long intervals without arrival, there were intervals that had far more arrivals than their even share. They are generally related to queue depth and request arrival rate and inter-arrival time. This phenomenon is often called long-range dependence and is typically explained as (stochastic) self-similarity because that is the only explanation that avoids non-stationarity. The phenomenon of self-similarity describes how a property of an object is preserved while scaling in space and/or in time. In other words, in addition to the long-range dependence property, the scale invariance property holds at any different time scale, like in a fractal shape.

Statistical Properties Visualization and Evaluation

Besides the statistical properties mentioned in previous sections, there are several other properties of both the marginal and the joint probability distributions of the interested attributes that may strong influence the quantitative analysis of the system behavior [35]:

- **Normality:** A probability distribution can be accurately approximated by a normal distribution. Although perfect normal distribution is rare in reality, it is often used a reference model.

- **Nonstationary:** In a stationary process, the outputs (job size, inter-arrival time) vary, but the stochastic process that produces them does not.

- **Long-tailness and power-law:** Some regions far from the mean or the median of the probability distribution, like the extreme values in the tails of the probability distribution, are assigned relatively high probabilities following a sub-exponential or polynomial law, contrary to what happens to the family of normal distributions, where the tails fall exponentially.

- **Heavy-tailness:** The long tails of the distribution fall polynomially and the self-similarity property holds.

- **Cyclic behavior and seasonal variations:** They are an indication of a non-stationary workload and must be treated separately.

- **Autocorrelation, cross-correlation, and short-range dependence:** Autocorrelation is also known as serial correlation or short-term/range memory, where the

autocorrelation at short time scales is significant and
long-range dependence is also known as long-term
memory, where the autocorrelation at long time scales
is significant.

These properties can be possibly visualized via graphical plotting. The
empirical cumulative distribution function (EDF) and the complementary
EDF (CEDF) are often used to observe the sample distribution. In
particular, the log-log EDF and log-log CEDF plots are usually applied
to compare the body and the tails of the sample probability distribution,
respectively. Similarly, the Q-Q plot (a plot of the quantiles of the first
data set against the quantiles of the second data set) can be employed
for evaluating possible differences, especially in the tails, between the
empirical probability distribution and another reference probability
distribution, either theoretical or empirical.

The mass-count disparity plot and the Lorenz curve can be used to
look for evidence of the power-law property. The mass-count disparity
plot displays the "mass" probability distribution (given by the probability
that a unit of mass belong to an item smaller than a predefined x) against
the "count" probability distribution (given by the CDF) in order to show
possible disparities between these two probability distributions. The
Lorenz curve is an alternative way to illustrate the relationship between the
"count" distribution and the "mass" distribution; it is generated by pairing
percentiles that correspond to the same value (i.e. a point (p_c, p_m) in the
curve is such that $p_m = F_m(x) = F_m\left(F_c^{-1}(p_c)\right)$ where $F_m(\cdot)$ and $F_c(\cdot)$ are the
cumulative distribution functions of the "mass" and "count" distributions,
respectively, and $F_c^{-1}(\cdot)$ is the inverse of $F_c(\cdot)$.

The run-sequence plot and the autocorrelation plot for investigating
for the presence of both short-range and long-range dependence as
long as for periodic patterns and trends. The run-sequence plot displays
observed data in a time sequence; it is constructed by plotting values of the
interested (univariate) attribute according to the temporal order as they

appear; this plot is particularly useful for finding both shifts in location and scale, for locating outliers and, in general, for getting insights about the trend of observed data. The autocorrelation plot (also known as a correlogram) is a plot of the sample autocorrelation function (ACF), which is of the sample autocorrelation at increasing time lags; it is used for checking for randomness in a sequence of observations of the same attribute. If random, such autocorrelations should be near to 0 for any and all time-lag separations; conversely, if non-random, then one or more of the autocorrelations will be significantly different from 0.

Some hypothesis-testing techniques can be used for quantitative evaluations of these properties, such as F-test, T-test, K-S (Kolmogorov-Smirnov) test, Mann-Whitney U-test, and H-test. These tests can compare the differences between two empirical distribution functions/samples. The Pearsons r and the Spearmans ρ correlation coefficients are utilized to discover linear and generic correlations, respectively, among the interested attributes. Both coefficients are within the range of $[-1,+1]$, where $+1$ means a strong positive correlation, while -1 means a strong negative correlation. 0 means no significant correlation. More details will be described in Chapter 9.

Read /Write Dependency

Dependencies are generally classified into four categories [39]:

- Read-on-write (ROW), or read after write (RAW), or true dependencies

- Write-on-write (WOW) or write after write (WAW) or write update, or output dependencies

- Write-on-read (WOR), or write after read (WAR), or anti-dependencies

- Read-on-read (ROR) or read cache hit, or input-dependencies

Within a certain time window, ROR and ROW are directly related to the cache replacement algorithm and read hit performance, while WOR and WOW are related to the cache update policy. The existence of a ROW between two operations relies on the situation that if the first operation writes a block that is later read by the other operation and there is no intervening operation on the block. WOW and WOR are similarly defined. ROR is a very common property to check read cache efficiency. ROW can check if the so-called "write once read many (WORM)" is possible, which is an important value for SMR (the higher the better).

Write Update (Write on Write)

A high WOW ratio generally means high block update ratio. Therefore, when replicate blocks exist, it might be better to update one of the copies and invalidate the remainder rather update all the copies, if the WOW ratio is quite high within a short time window, for IO performance consideration. By comparing ROW and WOW, you can conclude the likelihood of blocks getting updated vs. being read or not. SMR generally expects less write update, resulting in smaller write amplification. If an out-of-place policy is applied for write updates, you can expect better spatial efficiency.

In order to have a better view on WOW, I define three different types of update ratios below. Their different purposes are shown in Table 2-7.

Table 2-7. *Comparison of Write Update Ratios*

	Frequented	**Timed/ordered**	**Stacked**
Total updated blocks/commands	Yes	Yes	Yes
Timing issue	No	Yes	No
Update frequency	Yes	No	No
Memory stack	No	No	Yes

Frequented update ratio: During a time period, record the update frequency of each LBA. Any write hit is counted. If its frequency is larger than 1, the LBA is rewritten in the observation period. You can therefore provide a curve of x-axis vs. y-axis, where

- x is the maximum update frequency (≤ 1 no rewritten; otherwise rewritten)

- y is the percentage of blocks updated (updated blocks at a specified-frequency value / total updated blocks of write commands) or its cumulated distribution function (CDF).

This process gives a quick, coarse grain analysis of how LBAs are updated in a workload of conventional PMR drives. However, it may not reflect the actual ratio for SMR drives. In fact, due to the indirect mapping and log nature of SMR, it misses the actual write update; for example, a rewrite with an out-of-place update actually is "new" write to SMR drives.

Timed/ordered update ratio: During a time period, record the total blocks of updated write request (repeated or not). An update is an operation to rewrite a block that was previously written during the observation period. You can provide a curve of x = time or command IDs vs. y = total size of updated blocks or percentage of blocks updated (updated blocks at frequency x / total blocks of commands), so the percept is the percentage of total blocks that were updated. Note that a similar definition to frequented update ratio and timed/ordered update ratio are given in [4, 40].

Stacked update ratio: During a time period, record the update frequency of each write command (partial or full hit). Once a rewrite happens, it is counted as a new command (update frequency is always ≤ 1). You can provide a curve of x = logical stack distance vs. y = percentage of updated write commands (updated write commands/total commands), or a curve of x = logical stack distance vs. y = percentage of updated write size (updated write size/total commands). It shows the actual update size/ commands and tells if an update in SSD/DRAM cache is necessary. Note that the stack distance can be also replaced by time interval.

Read on Write (ROW)

This metric is used to check if "write once read many (WORM)" is possible. In general, the higher the ROW ratio, the better the WORM property of the workload.

Frequented ROW ratio: During a time period record the read hit frequency of each LBA after a write command. You can then plot a curve of x = maximum hit numbers or frequency (<1 not updated, otherwise updated) vs. y = percentage of blocks or commands hit (updated blocks at frequency x / total number of HDD blocks).

Timed ROW ratio: During a time period, record the hit blocks of each read command since last write. You can provide a curve of x = time or command ID vs. y = percentage of blocks or commands of read hit commands (blocks of hit read commands/blocks of total commands).

Stacked ROW ratio: During a time period, record the hit frequency of each read command (partial or full hit) since last write. You can provide a curve of x = logical stack distance vs. y = percentage of read hit command (hit read commands/total read commands) or y = percentage of blocks of read hit command.

Beyond the material presented here, other qualities, such as self-similarity (for burst IO) and workload dependence among of nodes (i.e. how the tasks are distributed among nodes) [35, 39], are interesting metrics to be studied further. In the spirit of brevity, I include a targeted presentation of workload metrics, omitting these analyses.

Priority-Related Metrics

Requests have priority during execution. Usually, the foreground activities have higher priority than background activities. In some cases, such as synchronization in RAID5/6 and EC operations, these marked as synchronized requests may have higher priority due to time-out policies.

Other metrics may be related to cluster, multi-threads, network and so on [41]. For example, the network factors (I/O bandwidth distribution, channel utilization, instructions, packet sizes, source or destination of packets, page reference pattern, various forms of delay like transfer time and queuing delays, etc.) will also influence the final device performance.

Modeling Issues

There are two regular approaches to evaluating a system design. One employs the traced workload directly to drive a simulation. The other builds a model from the trace and uses the model for either analysis or simulation. Although the numerical trace-based approach is straightforward, the workload models may have some advantages over traces, such as adjustment with controlled modification, repetitions, stationarity, generalization, avoiding noise, increased understanding, added features, efficiency, etc. Therefore, it is important to understand the metrics via mathematical models. In the previous section, I pointed out that the hypothesis tests are based on some assumptions of statistical models. Tables 2-8 and 2-9 list few common sense details on the modeling issues of some basic and advanced metrics. For more details, refer to [35].

Table 2-8. *Mathematical Models for Basic Metrics*

Metrics	Modeling issues
Throughput	Commonly used distributions: Pareto distribution
Queuing time	Commonly used distributions: exponential distribution, Erlang distribution
Service time	Commonly used distributions: exponential distribution, Erlang distribution
Response time	Commonly used distributions: exponential distribution, Erlang distribution
Disk seek time	May be modeled by data fitting using a piecewise function
Read to write ratio	No obvious distribution, depends on read/write dependency
Request size distribution	Commonly used distributions: logarithmic distribution, trunked-normal distribution, Pareto distributions, exponential distribution, power-law distribution, log-uniform
LBA range/ randomness	See spatial locality
Inter-arrival time	Commonly used distributions: Poisson distribution, exponential distribution, lognormal distribution

Table 2-9. *Mathematical Models for Advanced Metrics*

Metrics	Modeling issues
Locality	Commonly used distributions: Zipf distribution (Independent Reference Model). Other models: LRU stack model, Markovian models, fractal model
Spatial locality	The simplest way is by counting unique substrings of the reference stream. Formally measured by the size of the working set.
Temporal locality	The simplest measure is to look at the reference stream through a pinhole or using a simulation of an LRU stack.
Read/write dependency	Models: State machine, Markov chain, clustering
Priority-related metrics	They are completely determined by the OS/FS rules. A model can be built based on Markov chain with
Burstiness and self-similarity	Auto-covariance and covariance matrices are often used to describe self-similarity.

A general procedure to generate an analytical model is as follows:

- First, decide the formulation: the characterization level and the workload basic component.

- Second, collect the parameters of the workload to be modeled while it is executed.

- Third, statistically analyze the measured data with some statistical distribution (e.g., logarithmic distribution, trunked-normal distribution, Pareto distributions, exponential distribution, power-law distribution, log-uniform distribution) and stochastic model (e.g., Markov models), including the sampling procedure and static/dynamic analysis.

An example using Markov chain can be stated in the following steps.

1. Assuming the workload is approximately periodic
    with s states, model the IO trace of each data
    storage unit in one cycle as a specific Markov chain.
    Otherwise, all the corresponding Markov chain
    parameters should be time-varying.

2. Given a historic workload trace L, represented as a
    $D \times T$ matrix:

$$X = \begin{bmatrix} x_{1,1} & x_{1,2} & \cdots & x_{1,T} \\ x_{2,1} & x_{2,2} & \cdots & x_{2,T} \\ \cdots & \cdots & \cdots & \cdots \\ x_{D,1} & x_{D,2} & \cdots & x_{D,T} \end{bmatrix}$$

    where D is the total number of data storage units
    and T is the total number of time intervals. $x_{d,t}$ is the
    IO intensity for any chosen data unit d at time t.
    $x_{d,t} \in \{1, 2, 3, ..., s\}$.

3. Each Markov chain can be represented by its s by s
    state transition probability matrix:

$$P = \begin{bmatrix} p_{1,1} & p_{1,2} & \cdots & p_{1,T} \\ p_{2,1} & p_{2,2} & \cdots & p_{2,T} \\ \cdots & \cdots & \cdots & \cdots \\ p_{s,1} & p_{s,2} & \cdots & p_{s,s} \end{bmatrix}$$

    where $p_{i,j}$ is the probability of the data unit IO
    intensity state change to j at next time interval under
    the condition that its current IO intensity state is i,
    and $i, j \in \{1, 2, 3, ..., s\}$

4. To simplify data allocation in the tiered storage
    system, you also need to classify the thousands of
    data units into a dozen of data clusters according to
    their dynamic IO intensities, such as a K-means
    algorithm using the state transition probability
    matrices as well as the residual time for each state s
    of every data units. By combining the initial state of
    the cluster S, you can obtain the predicted IO
    intensity of all the clusters in a whole period,
    represented as the following $N \times T$ matrix:

$$S = \begin{bmatrix} s_{1,1} & s_{1,2} & \cdots & s_{1,T} \\ s_{2,1} & s_{2,2} & \cdots & s_{2,T} \\ \cdots & \cdots & \cdots & \cdots \\ s_{N,1} & s_{N,2} & \cdots & s_{N,T} \end{bmatrix},$$

where $s_{l,t}$ is the IO intensity of the lth data cluster at
the tth time interval.

Refer to [7, 8] to see the difference between simulation and modeling
approaches. For more complex cases, you may use the so-called multiple-
level process models. And, in these cases, the correlation must be
considered.

Typical Applications

In this section, you will take a look at several trace metrics of some typical
applications in order to get a quick view. Table 2-10 lists some typical
applications, where only block size, read/write percentage, and random/
sequential percentage are provided with some rough values. The dominant
factors, IOPS or MBPS (throughput), actually show that whether the
workload is random request dominant or sequential request dominant.

Table 2-10. *Typical Application IO Workload Profiles*

Application	Size (Byte)	R/W	Rand./seq.	Dominant
	Application IO profile			
Web file server	4KB, 8KB, 64KB	95%/5%	75%/25%	IOPS
Database online transaction processing (OLTP)	8KB	70%/30%	100%/0%	IOPS
Exchange email	4KB	67%/33%	100%/0%	IOPS
OS drive	8KB	70%/30%	100%/0%	IOPS
Decision support systems (DSS)	1MB	100%/0%	100%/0%	IOPS
File server	8KB	90%/10%	75%/25%	IOPS
Video on demand	512KB	100%/0%	100%/0%	IOPS
Web server logging	8KB	0%/100%	0%/100%	MBPS
SQL server logging	64KB	0%/100%	0%/100%	MBPS
OS paging	64KB	90%/10%	0%/100%	MBPS
Media streaming	64KB	98%/2%	0%/100%	MBPS

IO workload characteristics are generally application-dependent nature. Many access patterns, such as read/write proportions and handling of writes differ by particular applications. Nevertheless, the majority of characteristics vary only by environments (operating conditions). Environment-dependent characteristics include the length of idle intervals, request arrival rate, workload randomness and sequentially, read and write performance, disk service time and response time of request, request size, etc. More importantly, there are characteristics of the overall IO workload that do remain consistent through applications and environments. A particular note here is workload burstiness (i.e. long-range dependence). The block-level workloads, in particular, request inter-arrival times and request seek distances, are long-range–dependent in general. As a measure of temporal locality in a time series, long-range dependence has a variety of consequences specifically with regards to predict overall system and particular resource saturation. Consequently, burstiness shall be taken into consideration when designing new storage systems, and resource management policies at various layers of the IO path. As a result, there is no universally good configuration for all workloads due to large difference in various applications [42].

For file system performance, keeping the file system block size close to the workloads I/O size can increase the efficiency of the system significantly [43].

Web traffic volume is increasing rapidly. Some researchers argue that there have been no dramatic changes in web server workload characteristics in the last 10 years [44]. They consist of one-time referencing behaviors, heavy-tailed file size distributions, non-Poisson aggregate request streams, high concentration of references, Poisson per-document request streams, and the dominance of remote requests.

A database usually has a significant inter-transaction locality, showing that real workloads transactions are generally dependent of each other. Another observation is that significant use of sequential accesses allows a prefetch policy to be applied. Sequentiality is a consequence of long-running queries that examine a large number of records, such as a join operation.

OLTP (online transaction processing) workloads are characterized by a large memory footprint, joined with a small critical working set, and by their reduced benefit from micro-architectural optimizations. In addition, index searching in OLTP workloads require a different cache design.

Let's further look into two workloads with more details.[3] Table 2-11 show the metrics values of the two traces. You can see that their properties have large differences. Sometimes, only two or three major metrics are used in the simple synthetic trace generators, although the applications' actual trace is much more complex.

Table 2-11. *Basic Metrics for Two Typical Workloads*

Trace	Duration(s)	Traffic (G-B)	Total requests ($\times 10^6$)	Avg. R/W size (KB)	R/W traffic ratio	Random read ($\times 10^6$)	Random write ($\times 10^6$)
OLTP	43712	18.491	5.335	3.466	0.1820	0.955	2.99
Search engine	3151.3	16.369	1.055	15.509	8762.9	0.994	2.08e-4

Traces in File- and Object-Levels

The other two types of traces generally share many common properties with block-level traces. However, they have their unique features in some scenarios. Table 2-12 gives some metrics of file-level traces, which are different from those of block-level traces.

---

[3]OLTP is from Financial1.spc and search engine from WebSearch1.spc of UMASS Trace Repository at http://traces.cs.umass.edu/index.php/Storage/Storage

Table 2-12. *Some Metrics for File-Level Traces*

Metrics	Explanation
File types	A file system is utilized in one of several ways: as a long term storage for persistent data, as a repository for data too large to fit in the main memory, as the site of storage for executables, and for storing logs of system usage for accounting and monitoring. The metadata to user data ratio is an important index
File age	The age is defined as the time from its last reference.
File access duration	The time from open to close
User behavior model	Users generate the references that constitute the workload.
Process and state model	Several aspects are included, such as how a process makes file service requests during its existence; the conditional activation table for access dependency; and the ratio of different operations, such as open, close, write, read, seek, etc. It may be molded as a closed Markov chain.
Reference model	How the requests are distributed among the files in the system

As mentioned, the metrics to be considered may be different based on different abstract levels. For example, in the system level, we usually consider the attributes listed in Table 2-13, where most of them could be in file or object-levels.

Table 2-13. *Workload in System Level*

Workload in systems views	Load arrival pattern	Data access pattern	Computation pattern
MapReduce	The time arrival of sequence of jobs	HDFS input and output paths, the data size for the input, shuffle, and output storage	Input data size, shuffle data size, output data size, job duration, map task time, reduce task time
Enterprise network storage	The time arrival sequence of application instances or user sessions	Read/write, sequential/random, single/repeated access, file sizes, file types	N.A.

In this chapter, I presented some trace metrics for performance evaluation and design of storage systems. Some typical applications were given to provide a quick impression on these metrics. In fact, due to the large difference of some applications, there is no one-for-all system design in general. I will discuss more details in the later chapters.

CHAPTER 3

Trace Collection

Trace quality is one of the essential requirements for analysis. Low quality traces may lead to complex, wrong conclusions for trace analysis. There are two main issues in trace quality. One is timing drift, which is when the actual event arrival time is earlier than the collected arrival time. The other is a missing event, such as when the tool cannot capture all the required events. Thus, proper tools shall be applied to guarantee the correctness of the traces. Both software tools and hardware devices are introduced in this chapter.

Collection Techniques

Many techniques have been proposed to monitor and capture system or component traces. There are four techniques generally:

- Hardware-based monitoring entails the modification of the testbed hardware so that as a program is executed, a record of all instructions and/or data addresses is created.

- Software-based tracing can achieve similar goals as hardware to a certain degree, but instead of altering the system hardware, software is modified or inserted.

© Jun Xu 2018
J. Xu, *Block Trace Analysis and Storage System Optimization*,
https://doi.org/10.1007/978-1-4842-3928-5_3

- Emulation-based tracing constructs a layer between the host machine and the OS under evaluation, like QEMU[1] and SimOS.[2] The layer only emulates enough components to allow the OS to run correctly. While this system provides a flexible interface to collect operating system-dependent traces, the accuracy of the captured trace is dubious sometimes. Since emulation is performed, execution will be perturbed.

- Microcode-based tracing utilizes microcode modification to capture trace information, introducing minimal slowdown, like PALcode (Privileged Architecture Library code).[3]

However, the third and fourth techniques are not popular due to high complexity and dubious accuracy. Therefore, only hardware and software based techniques are discussed in this chapter.

Hardware Trace Collection

We refer the hardware method to the trace collection approach that uses a particular hardware device/system capturing the IOs other than the targeted storage devices, although some software may be still required to manage the traces [38, 45]. There are many types of hardware to collect the block-level trace. One of the most common devices is a bus analyzer, although it is not limited to block-level IOs for disk drives, such as network traffic, DDR/CPU caching/stall/latency/throughput/etc. Some products can capture rather accurate traces, such as the Xgig 6G SAS/SATA analyzer from Viavi solution, the BusXpert Micro II Series SAS/SATA analyzer from

---

[1]www.qemu.org/
[2]http://simos.stanford.edu/
[3]http://download.majix.org/dec/palcode_dsgn_gde.pdf

SerialTek, the Trace and analyzer from TI, the protocol analyzer from LeCroy, the Eumulator XL-100 from Arium, and the SuperTrace Probe from Green Hills Software.

The bus analyzers often provide multiple communication interfaces for users. Take the devices in Figure 3-1 as an example. They provide USB, Ethernet, SCSI, etc. These devices usually achieve reliable and accurate linkups via multiple mechanisms, with higher resolution (e.g., time precision and capture frequency) and more information captured than software-based tools.

Figure 3-1. *Bus analyzers from LeCropy, XGIG, and SerialTek*

Figure 3-2 shows an example of SAS IO access in BusXpert, which provides almost all basic information related to SAS protocols. The users can easily trace the command status from the detailed logs, such as the response time, connections, etc.

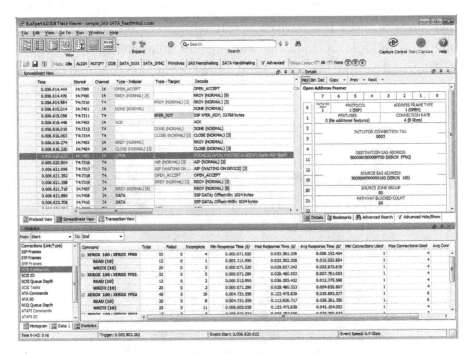

Figure 3-2. *Plentiful protocol information from BusXpert*

Figure 3-3 provides another example of SATA command analysis. You can see that the host issued the command COMWAKE after around 5 seconds. The drive almost immediately acknowledged COMWAKE. At time 5.59 seconds, SMART READ DATA was transferred to the host.

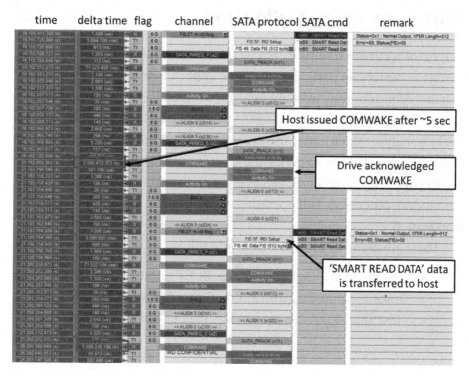

Figure 3-3. SATA command analysis

93

Although there is no difficulty in capturing almost all the essential protocol information, no advanced metrics of IO properties are included in the software used to analyze the trace.

Software Trace Collection

In term of accuracy, a software trace collector may be not as good as hardware devices. In particular, for these applications with time precision in nanoseconds or less, software may not work well. For example, a disk feature debug related to the SAS/SATA protocol may be applicable to the bus analyzer since it may involve the disk drive's SoC clock issues. However, for disk drive IO performance, it is generally operated at the millisecond level (precision), which is generally within the capability of the modern processors and operating systems inside a common server or workstation.

There are many IO tools available [45, 35]:

- Linux/Unix: Dtrace[46], LTTng, BCC,[4] iostat, dstat, tracefs,[5] iotop, hdparm, ionice, Ctrace,[6] iogrind, POSIX Test Suite, ioprofile, SystemTap, IOR, PCP, and swtrace

---

[4]https://github.com/iovisor/bcc

[5]www.usenix.org/conference/fast-04/tracefs-file-system-trace-them-all. It is a thin stackable file system used to capture file system traces in a portable way. Tracefs can capture uniform traces for any file systems without modifying the file systems being traced. It can also capture traces at various degrees of granularity: by users, groups, processes, file operations, files and file names, etc. In addition, it can transform trace data into aggregate counters, compressed, checksummed, encrypted, or anonymized streams; and it can buffer and direct the resulting data to various destinations (e.g., sockets, disks, etc.).

[6]http://ctrace.sourceforge.net/. CTrace is a fast and lightweight trace/debug library designed specifically for multi-threaded applications. It is coded in C and employs POSIX threads.

- Windows: Xperf,[7] TraceWPP/TraceView/Tracelog/
  Logman,[8] Vtrace, Oracle trace collector, Bus analyzer
  module,[9] and PatchWrx[10]

However, not all of these tools can provide event details. In fact, the general purpose monitoring tools, like iostat and iotop, cannot provide detailed information on a per-IO basis.

These tools can be divided into two classes: static and dynamic. Static tools view the binary image of a program as a black box that is never modified. Dynamic tools instead rely on binary-level alterations to facilitate the gathering of statistical data from an application. For example, all the Windows tools and iotop/iostat/dstat/hdparm/ionice/iogrind/ioprofile are static tools, while SystemTap, Dtrace, and LTTng are dynamic tools. In particular, Dtrace and LTTng use a mechanism called probing that is able to selectively activate instrumentation routines that are embedded within software at all levels of abstraction, so that performance-related statistics can be obtained from not only an application but also the various libraries and kernel routines associated with its execution.

---

[7]http://xperf123.codeplex.com/. Xperf is built on top of the ETW (Event Tracing for Windows) infrastructure, which provides the capability to capture event traces for user and kernel mode drivers.

[8]http://msdn.microsoft.com/en-us/library/windows/hardware/ ff552961(v=vs.85).aspx. These Windows tools enable WPP tracing in a trace producer and controlling trace sessions (trace controllers).

[9]www.scsitoolbox.com/products/BusAnalyzerModule.asp. BAM is a software bus analyzer that can capture, display, and analyze trace data from any peripheral bus, including SCSI, Fiber Channel, IDE, ATA, SATA, and SAS. BAM offers complete versatility as far as choice of phases that are captured and displayed, capture modes to minimize IO impact, buffer size and capture size, and device(s) to capture trace data from.

[10]http://studies.ac.upc.edu/doctorat/InstProf/PatchWrx.pdf. PatchWrx is a static binary-rewriting instrumentation tool to capture full instruction and data address traces on the DEC Alpha platform running Microsoft NT. The toolset modifies the binary image before execution.

Blktrace

Blktrace is a static tool that has been embedded into the Linux kernel since version 2.617-rc1. This tool is lightweight and easy to use. It only considers device access after OS/FS cache. When IO enters to block an IO layer (request queue), the relay channel per CPU gets events emitted, and blktrace then captures the events from the channels. More details can be found in Appendix B.

Dtrace, SystemTap, and LTTng

As mentioned, dynamic tracing tools embed tracing code into working user programs or kernels, without the need of recompilation or reboot. Since any processor instruction may be patched, it can virtually access any information you need at any place. I will discuss several dynamic tracing tools next.

DTrace [47] originated from Solaris.[11] Its development was begun in 1999, and it became part of the Solaris 10 release. Nowadays, DTrace is open-sourced as a part of OpenSolaris, although it has not merged into the Linux kernel due to license incompatibility. There exist several ports without proper support. A toolkit based on Dtrace for simplification of use has been developed by B. Gregg.[12] But the essential limitation has been solved. A few attempts led to the development of another clone of DTrace · called DProbes, but it seems to be unsuccessful.

Therefore, three major Linux players, Red Hat, Hitachi and IBM, presented another dynamic tracing system for Linux called SystemTap.[13] SystemTap is one of the most powerful tracers so far. However, it has to generate a native module for each script it runs, which is a huge

---

[11]www.solarisinternals.com/wiki/index.php/DTraceTopics
[12]https://github.com/opendtrace/toolkit
[13]http://sourceware.org/systemtap/langref/

performance penalty. Ktap[14] was further developed to reduce the overhead using Lua and LuaJIT internally. Another similar implementation is sysdig,[15] which is scriptless.

LTTng[16] is also a widely used open source tracing framework for Linux. It used static tracing and required kernel recompilation until version 2.0; it currently utilizes ftrace and kprobe subsystems in the Linux kernel. It makes the users understand the interactions among multiple system components, like the Linux kernel, using either existing or user-defined instrumentation points, C/C++ applications, Java applications, Python applications, or any other user space application with the LTTng logger. It may outperform other tracers because it has optimized event collection. It also supports numerous event types, including USDT (user-level statically defined tracing).

When identifying the overall system performance instead of only storage IO, these tools will play a significant role. In Chapter 9, you will use Ceph as an example to find the performance bottleneck from an overall system view.

Trace Warehouse

Mainly for research purposes, there are some real/synthesis traces available online for download. The following are few examples:

- SNIA at http://iotta.snia.org. It provides block IO trace (e.g., the block traces on a virtual desktop infrastructure and Microsoft Production Servers), NFS trace, system call trace, etc.

---

[14]https://github.com/ktap/ktap
[15]www.sysdig.org/
[16]http://lttng.org/

- Sandia National Laboratories at `www.cs.sandia.gov/Scalable_IO/SNL_Trace_Data/`. S3d I/O kernel trace data was collected during runs on 6400 clients of Redstorm.

- Los Alamos National Laboratory at `http://institute.lanl.gov/data/`. Few traces, like MPI/HPC, are categorized.

- Google at `https://github.com/google/cluster-data`. It provides cluster workload trace on Google compute cells.

- Facebook at `https://github.com/SWIMProjectUCB/SWIM/wiki/Workloads-repository`. A number of 1-hour segments from Facebooks Hadoop traces were published as part of UC Berkeley AMP Labs SWIM project.

- Dartmouth University at `www.cs.dartmouth.edu/dfk/nils/workload.html`. It provides some traces from parallel file systems (e.g., Intel's CFS, Thinking Machines SFS).[17]

- Harvard University at `www.eecs.harvard.edu/sos/traces.html`. It provides some NFS traces.

- UMassAmherst at `http://traces.cs.umass.edu/index.php/Main/Traces`. OLTP and search engine traces are archived.

---

[17]Most of these traces have been designed under the assumption that scientific applications running on parallel computers would exhibit behavior similar to that of the same applications running on uniprocessors and vector supercomputers.

- Hebrew University at `www.cs.huji.ac.il/labs/parallel/workload/index.html`. Multiple parallel workloads are collected.

- OpenCloud at `http://ftp.pdl.cmu.edu/pub/datasets/hla`. These traces were taken from a Hadoop cluster managed by CMU's Parallel Data Lab. They provide very detailed insights into the workload of a cluster used for scientific workloads during a 20-month period, including timestamps, slot counts, and more.

Together with the source code for the analysis tool, I also provide trace sample data in GitHub.

This chapter discussed both hardware and software tools for trace collection. Note that the former generally offer higher precision and more information than the latter, although they are more expensive. However, in many scenarios, the precision is only required at the millisecond level. Therefore, software-only tools are widely applied in both industries and academics. Note that there exist various tools for different purposes. In order to identify the overall system performance, you shall employ multiple tools or some integrated tool sets.

CHAPTER 4

Trace Analysis

Trace analysis provides insights into workload properties and IO patterns, which are essential for storage system tuning and optimizing. This chapter discusses how the workload interacts with system components, algorithms, structures, and applications.

Interactions with Components

As discussed in Chapter 1, different storage devices may have large different properties. In addition, their internal structures and algorithms also have significant impacts on the final performance. For example, write cache of HDDs can gain benefits from data locality:

- Write cache hits can avoid some disk mechanical writes; instead, the dirty blocks in DRAM cache are overwritten. It is a benefit of temporal locality.

- Larger cache space means longer write queue: physically contiguous dirty blocks can be grouped into a single IO operation. It is a benefit of spatial locality.

- An advanced replacement policy efficiently places cold data onto a disk while keeping the hot data in cache via exploring both spatial and temporal locality.

© Jun Xu 2018
J. Xu, *Block Trace Analysis and Storage System Optimization*,
https://doi.org/10.1007/978-1-4842-3928-5_4

- The cache can temporarily absorb the write burst and distribute the write load evenly over time to minimize the impact to concurrent IOs.

For HDD with MBC, write cache can provide log access for write burst, and thus give a better arrangement for grouped I/O access. In this section, I mainly discuss the HDD and SSD factors that influence the performance.

HDD Factors

For HDD, the performance varies with respect to (wrt) the disk drive's features (e.g., RPM, TPI/SPT, location [OD, MD or ID], head quality, servo control mechanism, cache structure/algorithm, queue length, and so on) and workload properties (e.g., sequence, request size, queue depth, and more).

First, look at drive's features. For example, the throughput of the OD side of HDDs can be double that of the ID side, as shown in Figure 4-1. A 10K RPM enterprise drive may be over two times faster than a 5400 RPM desktop drive. The fast RPM drives generally have a quicker response time than the slow RPM ones.

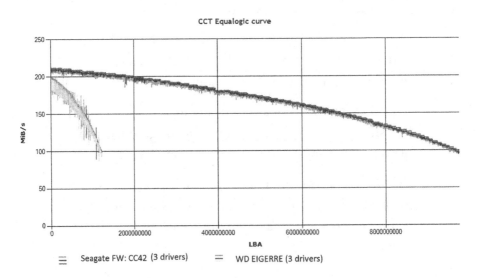

Figure 4-1. *Throughput difference in different HDD locations*

Second, consider the workload properties. Figure 4-2 provides an example that IOPS changes wrt request size (0.5, 1, 2,..., 2014KB) and queue depth (1, 2, 4, 8, 16, 32) for write cache enabled (WCE) or disabled (WCD). You can see that without cache/buffer, WCD gives similar performance for different queue depths under the same request size. However, when write cache is enabled, the performance for queue depth as 1 has a significant difference from that for 16. Figures 4-2 and 4-3 illustrate the performance difference wrt buffer size under WCE and WCD.

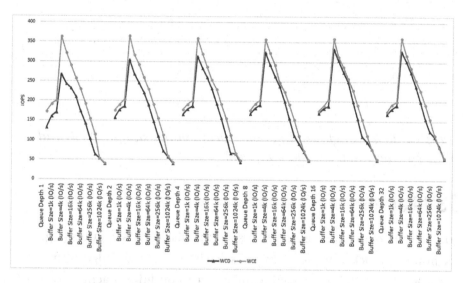

Figure 4-2. *IOPS difference wrt queue depth and request size under WCE and WCD (random write via IOMeter)*

103

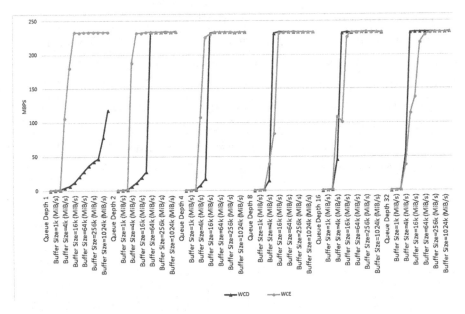

Figure 4-3. *Throughput difference wrt to buffer size for WCE and WCD (sequential write via IOMeter)*

SSD Factors

For SSD, the performance also varies wrt the disk drive's features (e.g., die number, block size, parallel access, flash management algorithm (wear-leveling), address mapping policy, trim condition, cache structure/ algorithm, queue length, IO driver interface, and more) and the workload properties (e.g., fragmentation, sequence/randomness, write update, read/ write ratio, request size, queue depth, request intensity/throttling, etc.).

Different from HDD, a consumer-class NAND SSD may show artificially and unsustainably high performance temporarily during initial measurements. It may also display unacceptable performance in bad conditions. Thus I shall have a proper condition for SSD in order to demonstrate sustained solid-state performance. The well-known starting point is a completely new SSD or a low-level formatted SSD (to wipe the contents and restore it to its original state). Run some random writes for a while, depending on the SSD capacity. Then the SSD is put in a "used" state. When the performance levels settle down to a sustainable rate, we have the true performance value. Figure 4-4 illustrates this phenomenon, where D1-D6 are MLC and D7-D8 are SLC.[1] Note that this situation has been alleviated since 2017.

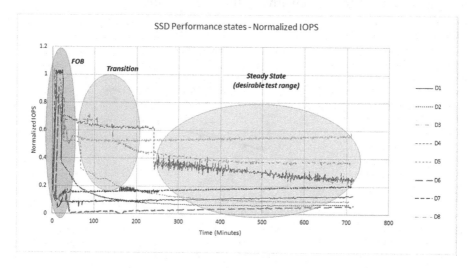

Figure 4-4. *SSD performance states [12]*

NAND SSDs generally use a virtual address mapping scheme, whereby LBAs are mapped to PBAs for some reason [12]. For instance, wear leveling algorithms allocate updated data to new cell locations to promote evenly distributed wear on the memory cells and thus improve the memory cell life or endurance. As a result, the SSD must keep track of the LBA-PBA affiliations. Similar to HDD, sequential operation may also be faster than random access when the data in the physical location is less fragmented.

---

[1] http://searchsolidstatestorage.techtarget.com/feature/
The-truth-about-SSD-performance-benchmarks

Similar to HDD, the queue depth (i.e., the number of the outstanding IOs) has a deep impact to the IOPS performance. Figure 4-5 illustrates the IOPS trends for four different models of SSDs under two applications: database and file server. You can see that the resulting IOPS are largely different. In addition, SSD2 performs better than SSD3 in the database, while worse in the file server. This indicates that the internal architecture and algorithm of a SSD is sensitive to the applications.

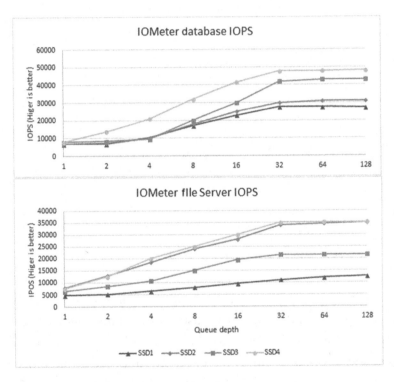

Figure 4-5. *SSD IOPS vs. queue depth*

Block alignment is also a performance issue. When blocks are aligned with the NAND flash memory cell boundaries, they are more efficiently stored in an SSD. For instance, an 8KB block will fit precisely in an 8KB NAND page size. If all things are equal, more small block IOs can be accessed in a given period of time than large block IOs, although the amount of data might be the same, such as 64 IOs of 8KB data transfer length vs. 4 IOs of 128KB data transfer length. In any case, the minimum granularity of access to NAND flash depends on the design of the underlying NAND flash. Figure 4-6 shows the throughput under sequential requests with different sizes. You can see that when the size is less than 32KB, the transfer speed is significantly influenced by the size. However, when the size is larger than 128KB, the throughput is relatively stable.

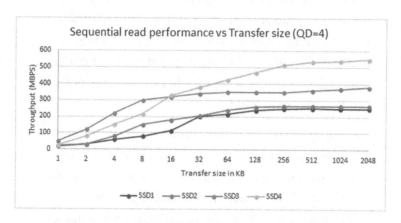

Figure 4-6. *SSD sequential throughput vs. request size*

The read/write ratio has larger impact to the SSDs than CMR HDDs. First, the "new" write generally needs more time than read, so more steps of the write operation than that of the read operation. Second, for a write-in-place update, an "erase" access is required. Therefore, the number of write steps relies on how full the drive is and whether the SSD controller shall erase the target cell (or even relocate some data by performing a more time-costly RMW access) before writing the new data.

Although the performance ratio of sequential to random access is not so high as the HDDs, sequentiality is still important because it contributes in minimizing erase operations via grouping write requests by blocks, optimizing both lifetime and I/O performance by reducing the number of erasures, and so on.

In sum, there are many major differences between SSD and HDD, besides those listed in the summary table in Chapter 1. Here, I further extend it to general NVM:

- **Access location**: It significantly matters for HDD due to positioning time, while it doesn't determine latency in NVM generally, although the access order matters.

- **Access size**: Large and sequential requests are significantly faster than small and random requests. However, it has less impact to NVM. In fact, larger IO may pay an additional cost due to internal structures, although sequential access is still generally faster than random access in NVM.

- **Access type**: HDD is usually either block- or file-based. Some object-based devices still use internal mapping between block and object. However, some NVMs can be byte-level. The object-level mapping is also more native than that of HDD. Read and write performances are likely to be different in many NVMs.

- **Content**: Some techniques, such as compression and reduplication, are content-dependent. They are not necessary for HDD due to the additional computational and IO resource usage, which may downgrade the HDD performance largely. Compared with the space saving, they may not be worthwhile. However, for NVM, these techniques can reduce the cost and improve the storage efficiency.

- **Timing**: HDD usually caps at 300 IOPS, while some NVM devices may be 100 to 10000 times faster. The cache scheduler therefore has large difference.

There are many testing and benchmarking tools with different measurement conditions. People may be confused by the results from these different tools. SNIA developed standard testing tools called SSSI Reference Test Platform (RTP) and the Performance Test Specification (PTS).[2]

Interactions with Algorithms

The algorithms and policies utilized in the hybrid storage systems actually determine the performance of the overall storage system when the hardware is fixed. In this section, the most important algorithms, such as data allocation, hot data identification, data migration, and scheduling algorithm, are surveyed. For easy of representation, I list some main factors considered in these algorithms in Tables 4-1 and 4-2, where access frequency and interval are the most important two factors in hot data identification and data migration algorithms.

Table 4-1. *Two Most Important Factors*

Items	Description	Typical Algorithms
Access frequency (R/W) (F), Access interval (T)	The access time within a given time period. Due to the different performance in R/W, we may also consider them separately. Some argue that the least recently used data may have higher probability to be re-accessed in the near future; some deny it; now an acceptable tradeoff is that it depends on IO pattern/workload.	LFU (least frequently used) [48], GDSF (Greedy-Dual Size Frequency) [49] LRU (least recently used), MRU (most recently used), LFUDA (LFU with dynamic aging) [48], LRU-K(least recently used k)[50], GDS [51]

---

[2]www.snia.org/forums/sssi/rtp

Table 4-2. *Other Performance Factors*

Items	Description
Data size	Generally, only hot data with small size is required to move to a higher tier. The small degree depends on the read/write speed rate of SSD and HDD, and the migration speed between them, etc.
Cache total/remaining size	The cache size decides how much hot data can be stored in the cache. Hence it decides the threshold of hot degree.
Device total/remaining bandwidth	The bandwidth decides if the migration is proper at current time. An approximated function may be built to predict the remaining bandwidth with respect to R/W ratio, IO intensity, etc.
R/W ratio	Since the R/W access time and pattern are different, this ratio gives different performance (e.g., the write amplification).
R/W granularity and IO intensity	The value represents the data amount ratio relating to an R/W IO to a fixed size data block. Average R/W granularity is the average ratio of all the IOs in a predefined time interval. Commonly, the larger the value, the more important the data is to users.

(continued)

Table 4-2. (*continued*)

Items	Description
Data correlation	One data may be related to another, so the IO operations in a data block have some characteristics in a predefined period of time, and another may have similar properties, hence they are associated. This value can be used for IO predication.
IO range/amount/distribution	IO distribution represents the statistical accessing information, such as the accessing address range and the accessing frequency in a given accessing period.
Grain size	The minimum size for each page/block to be replaced/migrated
Tier contrast/compensation (device value)	It values the difference between two different storage tiers/caches for direct data migration, including device status, accessing speed, etc.
Others	Data loss/error, etc.

Interactions with Structure

The fundamental structure of the storage device or system also has a large impact on the system performance. For example, RAID- and EC-based systems have the functionality of data protection. However, it increases the internal IO burden to the disks due to the additional parity data. In particular, during the system recovery from a critical disk failure, the internal workload eats large portion of disk bandwidth, and therefore the overall system performance to the external users is significantly downgraded. Chapter 7 will analyze the impact of RAID structure to the IO pattern.

For a hybrid storage system, although it has the potential to improve the performance of hot data, the internal data migration may also occupy some additional resources. Improper IO scheduler and data migration algorithms will definitely lower the overall performance. In addition, the so-called cache structure and tiering structure may have large difference in data allocation and IO scheduling, which leads to performance diversity under different scenarios. Chapter 6 will use a small-scale hybrid device as an example. Furthermore, the inter-connection structure, such as bus and bridge, could also be the performance bottleneck in some cases.

Interactions with Applications

As discussed in Chapter 2, the metrics of different applications may have large differences [35]. Table 4-3 provides a simple comparison of typical requirements among some common applications.[3] Due to the significant variation of requirements from one to another, it imposes different demands on the storage systems. Chapter 8 will illustrate the IO pattern of a Hadoop system with HDFS for big data applications, while Chapter 9 will discuss one of the most popular distributed storage systems, Ceph.

---

[3]For space saving, the words "sequential," "performance," and "throughput" are shortened as "seq.", "perf." and "TP", respectively. Jie Yu and Grant Markey also contributed this table.

Table 4-3. *Typical Requirements for Some Applications*

	HPC data storage	Cloud Storage	HDFS/Mixed	Archive/Backup	HPC check pointing data	Database
Attribute	Near term data storage: Seq., high-TP WORM operations	Traditionally batch IO seq. read/write	Traditionally batch IO seq. read/write	Write once, read infrequently	Checkpoint operations: Bursty, high-TP operations	Transactional: Small IO read, modify write
Latency	Similar demands of cloud storage. Generally Ethernet, sometimes IB.	Between 10 and 100ms	Between 10 and 100ms	High latency expected (ι=10s); Amazon glacier at 3-5 hours	1-2 ms; up to 45us for >1kb data transfers	Faster the better, 0-10ms but can be 90ms before issues

(continued)

113

Table 4-3. (*continued*)

	HPC data storage	Cloud Storage	HDFS/Mixed	Archive/ Backup	HPC check pointing data	Database
IOPS/Tput	Many different offerings. Vendor-specific storage specs vary.	100s to 10k IOPS depending on size of instance	Disk perf. dependent, little observable overhead to impede HW perf.	LTO4 tape is 120MB/s with 22s latency	10K+ IOPS per 4U unit System performance usually;	Usually 1K-30K IOPS, up to 1-10M+ level; implementation is platform-specific;
Other	Usually for scientific data analysis, not super computer checkpoint storage.	High availability (4/5 of 9); high data durability (9/11 of 9)	In-place data analysis capability	High data durability is expected with infrequent data access	Communicates over dedicated IB 84.8TB per shelf	Supports ACID semantics

CHAPTER 5

Case Study: Benchmarking Tools

Benchmark tools are useful to provide some "standard" performance indexes for storage systems with specific requirements. This chapter shows how to identify the access pattern of benchmark results. The first tool is SPC-1C from the Storage Performance Council (SPC). After capturing the pattern, I developed a synthetic emulator to match the real traces. The second tool is PCMark from FutureMark. I illustrate how to use gain-loss analysis to improve cache algorithm efficiency.

Storage performance benchmarks assess the relative performance of storage systems by running a number of standards tests and trails, via a tool or a set of programs with or without specific hardware equipment supported. Below are some benchmark tools that are often used for active trace collection:

- Synthetic trace

    - The user can specify test scenarios for queue depth, request size, transfer rate, sequence, etc. It is good to determine corner case behavior.

    - Examples: IOMeter, VDBench, fio, IOzone, iorate, sqlio, diskspd[1].

---

[1]https://gallery.technet.microsoft.com/DiskSpd-a-robust-storage-6cd2f223

© Jun Xu 2018
J. Xu, *Block Trace Analysis and Storage System Optimization*,
https://doi.org/10.1007/978-1-4842-3928-5_5

- Application-based trace

    - The user can choose specific applications with predefined workload patterns. It is good to illustrate real world cases.

    - Examples: SysMark,[2] PCMark, SPC (Storage Performance Council, e.g., SPC-1, SPC-2), TPC (Transaction Processing Council, e.g., TPC-A/B/C/D/H/W),[3] SPEC (Standard Performance Evaluation Corporation, e.g., HPC/SFS/JVM/SDM),[4] Jetstress,[5] COSbench[6].

- Real trace

    - The user can input the real-world trace directly. It is useful when the user attempts to test similar applications in different systems.

    - Example: AnandTech Storage Bench[7].

Table 5-1 gives a simple comparison of some commonly used tools, where the letters W, L, and U in the OS column indicate Windows, Linux, and Unix, respectively.

---

[2]https://bapco.com/products/sysmark-2014/
[3]www.tpc.org/
[4]www.spec.org/
[5]www.microsoft.com/en-us/download/details.aspx?id=36849
[6]http://lbs.sourceforge.net/
[7]www.anandtech.com/

Table 5-1. *A Comparison of Some Common Benchmark Tools*

	Block	File	Posix	OS	S/C	Open	Latest
Iometer	Y	-	-	WLU	S/C	Y	1.1.0/ 2014
IOzone	Y	Y	Y	WLU	S	Y	2006
Bonnie++	Y			LU	S	Y (GPL2)	1.0.1
dbench	Y	Y	Y	LU	S/C	Y (GNU)	2008
Filebench	Y	Y	Y	LU	S	Y	2011

For large-scale systems, the traditional tools may be insufficient (e.g., lack of measurement metrics) or inconvenient (e.g., no integrated user interface) enough. Therefore, some dedicated tools are proposed, such as HiBench,[8] Berkely BDB,[9] BigDataBench,[10] and BigBench[11] for big data benchmarks, in particular, the Hadoop/Spark systems.

A general benchmark procedure is shown in Table 5-2 [52]. Note that there exist other classification methods. For example, three types are named as micro-benchmark in lower-level system operation (e.g., evaluating HDFS operations on modern cluster), functional/components benchmarks in high-level functions (e.g., Terasort, basic SQL), application-level benchmarks (e.g., overall system performance for a given application scenario). For more details, refer to [41, 35].

---

[8]https://github.com/intel-hadoop/HiBench
[9]https://amplab.cs.berkeley.edu/benchmark/
[10]http://prof.ict.ac.cn/BigDataBench/
[11]https://github.com/intel-hadoop/Big-Data-Benchmark-for-Big-Bench

Table 5-2. *Five Steps for General Benchmarks*

Steps	Remarks
Choose the proper configuration.	Select the proper type of benchmark, such as macro-benchmark (overall test for the full system), micro-benchmark (few operations to check partial changes), or trace-based.
Choose the correct environment.	Consistent hardware and software settings, and some factors, such as cache status, HDD zoned constant angular velocity, file system aging, nonessential processes, etc.
Run the benchmark.	Identical run for repeatability, multiple rounds for accuracy with small standard deviations or high confidence level, sufficient running time for steady state, automatic run via suitable scripts.
Present the results.	Statistical results with small confidence-interval and near normal distribution
Validate the results.	Reproduce/confirm the results or compare with other similar ones.

SPC-1C

The Storage Performance Council (SPC) provides several benchmarking tools under different levels. SPC-1C [53] is designed to be vendor/platform independent and is applicable for a wide range of storage component products, such as disk drives, host bus adapters (HBAs), intelligent enclosures, and storage software such as logical volume managers.

Workload Properties

Two important concepts related to the workload intensity are the BSU (business scaling unit) and ASU (application storage unit). Each BSU is composed of three ASUs: ASU1 for a data store with a weight of 45%, ASU2 for a user store with 45%, and ASU3 for a log with 10%, which totally corresponds to five IOPS per ASU.

There are three types of access patterns: random (uniform distribution), sequential, and (random walking access) pattern. The details can be found in Table 5-3, which is further summarized in Table 5-4. Table 5-5 indicates that the small size requests (8 and 16 blocks) are over 85%. Random walk is an important model of Markovian Chain. Table 5-6 shows the main characteristics of this model.

Table 5-3. *Decomposition of SPC-1C Workload*

ASU	1-1	1-2	1-3	1-4	2-1	2-2	2-3	3-1
Intensity	0.035	0.281	0.07	0.21	0.018	0.07	0.035	0.281
R/W	0.5	0.5	1	0.5	0.3	0.3	1	0
Random	1	0	0	0	1	0	0	0
Pattern	0	1	0	1	0	1	0	0
Seq.	0	0	1	0	0	0	1	1
Ratio	1-1	1-2	1-3	1-4	2-1	2-2	2-3	3-1
R rand.	0.0175	0	0	0	0.0054	0	0	0
R seq.	0	0	0.07	0	0	0	0.035	0
R pattern	0	0.1405	0	0.105	0	0.021	0	0
W rand.	0.0175	0	0	0	0.0126	0	0	0
W seq.	0	0	0	0	0	0	0	0.281
W pattern	0	0.1405	0	0.105	0	0.049	0	0

Table 5-4. *SPC-1C Workload Ratio*

Workload ratio	ASU1	ASU2	ASU3
ASU i/total	0.596	0.123	0.281
Read rand. in ASU i	0.02936	0.0439	0
Read seq. in ASU i	0.11745	0.28455	0
Read pattern in ASU i	0.41191	0.17073	0
Write rand. in ASU i	0.02936	0.10244	0
Write seq. in ASU i	0	0	1
Write pattern in ASU i	0.41191	0.39837	0

Table 5-5. *Size Distribution*

Size distribution	Probability	Size distribution	Probability
8	0.7684	64	0.03088
16	0.09264	128	0.03088
32	0.0772		

Table 5-6. *SPC-1C Random Walk Pattern*

ASU	1-1	1-2	1-3	1-4	2-1	2-2	2-3	3-1	Sum
Read	0	0.1405	0	0.105	0	0.021	0	0	0.2665
Write	0	0.1405	0	0.105	0	0.049	0	0	0.2945

You can also find from Table 5-7 that the write accesses and pattern access are dominate, which shows the importance of self-similarity and write cache in the benchmarking test.

Table 5-7. *Basic IO Pattern Distribution*

R/W	Ratio	Mode	Ratio
Read	0.3944	Random	0.053
Write	0.6056	Sequential	0.386
		Pattern	0.561

Synthetic Trace

With all these parameters, you can actually write your own synthetic trace generator. Thus more flexibility is provided to change any parameters you are interested in, such as disk size, BSU, simulation times, even the configuration of SPC-1C, like ASU, IOPS per BSU, distribution patterns, etc. For example, you can separate ASU from BSU to see the influence of different applications (data store, user store, and log./seq. write) instead of mixed workload, and change the distribution (e.g., inter-arrival time, request size, etc.) to fit more specific requirements. In addition, you may integrate the generator to another toolkit, such as Disksim [54] and IOMeter, as a synthetic generator component. Figures 5-1, 5-2, and 5-3 show the comparison of a real trace captured by bus analyzer and the synthetic trace generated by the MATLAB-based tool in Appendix A.

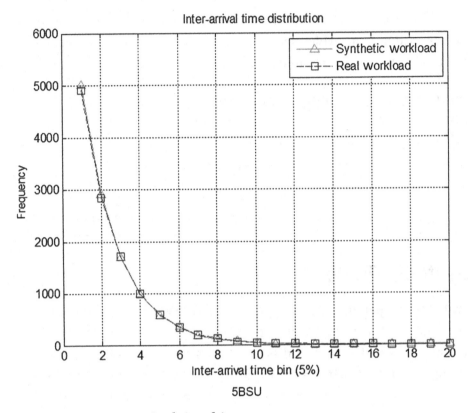

Figure 5-1. *Inter-arrival time histogram*

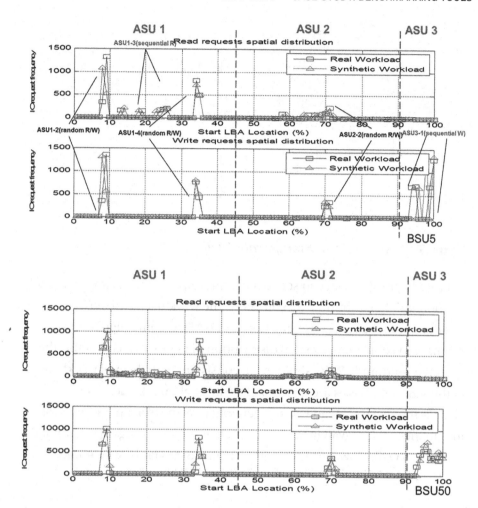

Figure 5-2. *SPC-1C spatial distribution*

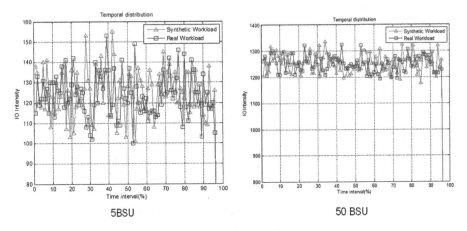

Figure 5-3. *SPC-1C trace temporal distribution*

From Figure 5-1, you can see that the inter-arrival time is approximately an exponential distribution. As you know, the workload is mixed by eight different types of IO streams from three ASUs. Some high intensity-streams are visible in this spatial distribution of Figure 5-2. Generally, the generated random R/W IO streams are consistent with the real workload, but the sequential ones are not very close in a light workload. One possible reason is the real workload was not generated by the exact parameters as those in the random walking model. In fact, it is hard to align the temporal distribution well. However, the result in Figure 5-3 is fairly acceptable.

PCMark

PCMark Vantage [55] is a widely used benchmark tool that is not limited to disk performance. It can provide application-level traces in eight categories, as shown in Table 5-8, where a particular trace is decomposed into the number of write and read commands. Figure 5-4 further shows the traces in the plot of LBA vs time.[12]

---

[12]Junpeng Niu helped part of coding work in this section.

Table 5-8. *Eight Applications in PCMark*

Order	Eight Apps	Total CMD	Write	Read
1	Windows Defender	6755	300	6455
2	Gaming	11040	62	10978
3	Importing Pictures	2806	4	2802
4	Vista Startup	7418	1327	6091
5	Video Editing	8204	3711	4493
6	Windows Media Center	5011	3309	1702
7	Adding Music	3336	1506	1830
8	Application Loading	11155	2660	8495

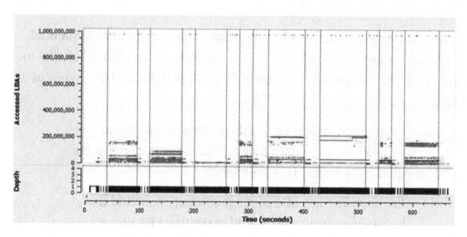

Figure 5-4. *Eight applications in PCMark*

Now you can use this trace as an example for the read cache performance analysis. Some early research shows that the common differentiator between drives is read cache hit rate, with reasonable pre- and/or post-read data. For easy of notation, I define a prefetch action as both a pre-read and post-read request, as shown in Figure 5-5. A common case is that some later read requests hit the data in the cache due to prefetch data, if the trace has a strong locality. Three types of prefetch accesses are commonly used: prefetch always (PA), prefetch on a miss (PoM), prefetch on a hit (PoH).

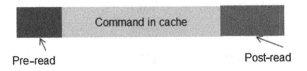

Figure 5-5. *Cache prefetch*

As mentioned, a gap between requests is allowed for near sequential streams. This gap can be a "hole" in the prefetch data, which is harmful to the overall performance. As shown in Figure 5-6, there are three types of holes:

- Post hole: The first LBA of the incoming command has a distance (> 0) within a threshold to the last LBA of the queued commands in the cache.

- Pre hole: The last LBA of the incoming command has a distance within a threshold to the first LBA of the queued commands in the cache.

- Pre and post hole: Both post and pre holes exist.

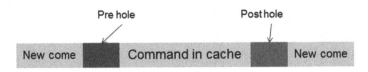

Figure 5-6. *Hole types*

To formally define the hole, consider the following two cases:

- **Constant:** If the range between two close regions in the cache is less than the constant Hs blocks, this range is viewed as a hole.

- **Adaptive:** The hole size is related to DRAM and SSD cache (most likely monotone increasing to the total/remaining

$$H_S = \begin{cases} \underline{H_S}, & \lfloor a_T S_T + a_R S_R \rfloor < \underline{H_S} \\ \overline{H_S}, & \lfloor a_T S_T + a_R S_R \rfloor > \overline{H_S} \\ \lfloor a_T S_T + a_R S_R \rfloor, & \text{Otherwise} \end{cases}$$

where S_T and S_R are the total and remaining cache size, respectively, and a_T and a_R are coefficients for S_T and S_R. An example for 64MB of DRAM cache is defined as

$$H_S = \begin{cases} 16, & \lfloor a_T S_T + a_R S_R \rfloor < \underline{H_S} \\ 256, & \lfloor a_T S_T + a_R S_R \rfloor > \overline{H_S} \\ \lfloor a_T S_T + a_R S_R \rfloor, & \text{Otherwise} \end{cases}$$

where $a_T = \dfrac{1}{2^{13}}, a_R = \dfrac{15}{2^{13}}$. The actual $\underline{H_s}$ and $\overline{H_s}$ are decided by trace, such as the median size of requests within a time window. More specifically, consider if the hole is in the same track/cylinder.

A background task shall be implemented to monitor the LBA regions in cache and the hit density on these regions. This process is also tasked to look for gaps in regions of data with some level of hit density and to generate self-induced read commands to fill in these holes with data from main store.

To connect the cache algorithm to the trace properties, use the following hypothesis:

- If two regions of a certain range within a time-frame have a high enough correlation, the gap between them is likely to be accessed.

- The pre-fetch should not affect the overall performance much, so the benefits gained from the additional cache hit ratio should be larger than the additional cost due to pre-fetch.

- The up-bound of the hole size to be fetched is decided by multiple factors, such as the total/remaining cache size, workload size, cache type, access time, etc.

Now we have some questions to answer.

- What is the benefit from a hole filling policy? The key is to get the increased cache hit ratio (hit ratio with hole filling v.s. hit ratio without hole filling).

- What is the additional cost from a hole filling policy? The key is to find how many self-induced commands are generated to fill the hole. The time of the user workload must be considered.

- Since the similarity exists between hole filling and the prefetch policy, is it possible to merge hole filling to prefetch policy (integration)? The key is to find the overlapped cache hit between two policies; if the overlap rate is high, prefetch may include hole filling as part of it.

- When and where to apply the two policies (or integrated policy) with balanced benefit and cost? The key is to reduce the additional mechanical access cost and cache pollution.

Workload Properties

Let's look at the think time and completion time first, as shown in Figures 5-7 and 5-8, respectively. You can see the large difference for their distributions of various applications. Table 5-9 further gives the mean and standard derivative values together with IOPS. Figure 5-9 and Table 5-10 provide the size distribution. You may also find the relation between the size and completion time.

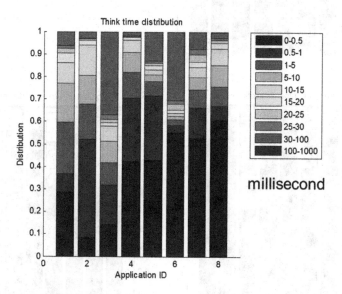

Figure 5-7. *PCMark: Think time distribution*

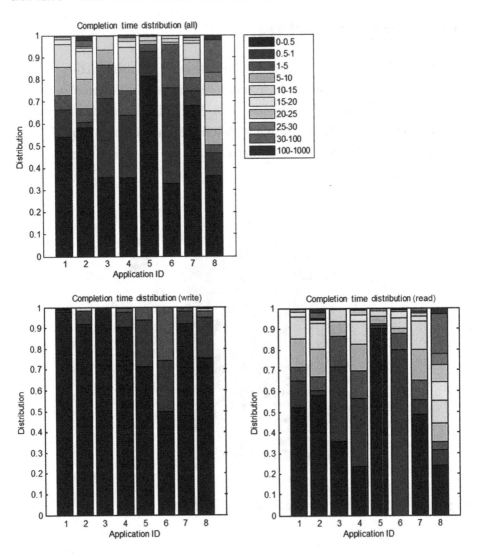

Figure 5-8. *PCMark: Completion time*

Table 5-9. *PCMark: Think/Completion Time (ms) and IOPS*

App	IOPS	Think-time mean	Std.	Completion-time mean (blk)	Std.
1	120.57	8.29	46.04	3.43	5.49
2	189.29	5.28	9.20	10.24	47.4
3	48.70	20.54	21.25	1.99	3.44
4	311.30	3.21	8.25	3.59	5.84
5	122.47	8.17	16.68	0.76	2.64
6	59.56	16.79	22.58	1.2	3.22
7	145.65	6.87	14.87	2.78	5.86
8	204.29	4.90	16.37	16.41	29.87

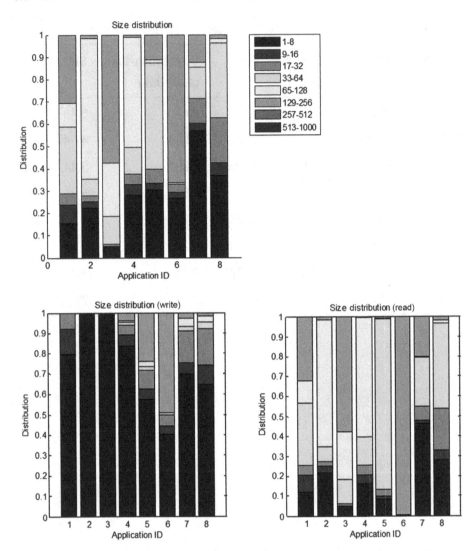

Figure 5-9. *PCMark: Size distribution*

Table 5-10. *PCMark: Size Distribution (Blocks)*

App	Mean -all	std.	Mean -read	std.	Mean -write	std.
1	98.67	87.55	102.78	87.4	10.22	7.3
2	86.92	56.39	87.36	56.24	8	0
3	175.09	82.28	175.33	82.1	8	0
4	71.92	54.86	83.12	49.32	20.48	49.35
5	60.77	63.68	59.18	25.42	62.69	90.43
6	173.36	115.82	255.16	13.43	131.29	122.52
7	43.01	61.43	60.39	70.63	21.89	38.54
8	36.23	37.58	41.31	37.47	20.04	33.11

Based on a sequential stream, you can observe some obvious sequences in general. Importing pictures has the most sequence, while application loading has less sequence. Except for application loading (mixed streams), queue length 10 is good enough to detect most streams. Application loading has relatively more mixed sequential streams. Also note that for read-only cases, most streams have only two commands. In Apps 2, 3, and 4, the average stream length is longer than others, which provides more chance for infinity read mode.

Gain-Loss Analysis

With the prefetch policy, the gain is from the increased hit ratio due to the cache policy (e.g., hole filling, prefetch), while the loss is from the additional disk access (e.g., pre-/post read attached to the user commands; the self-induced non-attached commands) due to the cache policy.

Two methods can be used to analyze the gain and loss. One simple method considers frequency only, so it counts the number of the hit frequency and additional disk access frequency. The self-induced commands' cost is generally smaller than non-attached commands. If the hit increases due to self-induced commands, the gain is large; otherwise, it is small. This method can provide a rough estimation. The other method is the so-called mixed simulation and modeling approach; it uses simulation to get the hit ratio and additional command frequency, while using the analytical model to obtain the average response time, which is relative complex and quantitative. Let's only consider the first one.

Let's define gain and loss quantitatively:

- **Gain:** The additional cache hit obtained (a_2) = the cache hit ratio at hole length x (a_3) - the cache hit ratio without hole filling (a_0)

- **Loss:** The additional self-induced commands occurrence / the total read command (a_1)

- **Gain-loss-ratio $a = a_2/a_1$:** The higher, the better to estimate a, but there are a few basic considerations:

  - **The queue depth (Q_d) in the cache:** which has significant influence on the LRU algorithm. By observing the largest a vs. Q_d, you will see that the optimal Q_d. Q_d for different applications may be various.

  - **The time interval (d_T) between commands:** Only if the interval is larger than a certain value, the system has chance to handle self-induced command, such as finding the ratio a for different d_T.

- **The hit frequency of each hole:** When using a correlation method to select the hole to fill, the hit frequency must be higher than 1. If the hit frequency is generally larger than 1, then this method is meaningful; otherwise, it is meaningless.

Let's start to verify whether a self-induced hole filling policy is beneficial. Take the following steps:

1. Check a_1, a_2, and a for all read commands (write commands also fill the cache).

2. If a_1 is much larger than a_2 (e.g., $a < 0.2$), it is not economic for hole filling; then check if a_2 is too small to be worthy. Otherwise, hole filling is useful; and check the selective self-induced commands based on workload.

3. If the time-interval between two commands is large enough (e.g., > 15ms), the self-induced command may not cost additional resources. If so, any increased cache hit ratio is beneficial. Repeat Steps 1-2.

Table 5-11 provides the results where Q_d = queue depth and f_s = filling hole size. You can see that App 2 is most significant for hole filling, while App 6 is least significant. Hole filling is generally suitable for Apps 2, 3, 5, and 8. If you only consider the commands with a think time larger than 10ms, you have the results listed in Table 5-12. You can see that the general trend is similar to the case without time-interval constraints. App 5 is most significant for hole filling for f_s = 128 and App 3 for f_s = 256; while App 6 is less significant. In sum, a is generally smaller than 1 for short queue depth. When hole size is very small, a is very small (<< 1). When both queue length and hole size are short, hole filling policy is generally useless. Based on the value of a, you can say that this policy is generally useless for App 6 and may be useful for Apps 2, 5, and 8. Further conclusion should be made after comparing with prefetch policy.

Table 5-11. *Gain-Loss Analysis for Hole Filling*

$Q_d=128; f_s=128$								
	1	2	3	4	5	6	7	8
a_2	0.026	0.024	0.007	0.001	0.049	0.000	0.051	0.079
a_1	0.328	0.060	0.041	0.183	0.099	0.020	0.293	0.192
a	0.078	0.399	0.165	0.007	0.494	0.000	0.175	0.413
$Q_d=128; f_s=256$								
	1	2	3	4	5	6	7	8
a_2	0.045	0.044	0.017	0.003	0.061	0.000	0.109	0.118
a_1	0.362	0.058	0.028	0.225	0.106	0.026	0.265	0.235
a	0.124	0.760	0.620	0.015	0.580	0.000	0.412	0.505
$Q_d=256; f_s=128$								
	1	2	3	4	5	6	7	8
a_2	0.029	0.034	0.007	0.003	0.048	0.000	0.051	0.102
a_1	0.338	0.065	0.042	0.183	0.099	0.031	0.295	0.206
a	0.084	0.520	0.160	0.014	0.490	0.000	0.174	0.493
$Q_d=256; f_s=256$								
	1	2	3	4	5	6	7	8
a_2	0.048	0.057	0.017	0.006	0.062	0.000	0.110	0.154
a_1	0.375	0.061	0.030	0.225	0.104	0.042	0.282	0.242
a	0.128	0.930	0.590	0.027	0.593	0.000	0.390	0.637

Table 5-12. *Gain-Loss Analysis for Hole Filling (Constrained)*

$Q_d=128; f_s=128$

	1	2	3	4	5	6	7	8
a_2	0.015	0.023	0.006	0.001	0.023	0.000	0.031	0.058
a_1	0.205	0.043	0.016	0.025	0.028	0.009	0.174	0.146
a	0.073	0.548	0.364	0.026	0.811	0.000	0.176	0.396

$Q_d=128; f_s=256$

	1	2	3	4	5	6	7	8
a_2	0.026	0.035	0.015	0.002	0.034	0.000	0.050	0.094
a_1	0.252	0.045	0.006	0.041	0.037	0.014	0.196	0.184
a	0.105	0.778	2.389	0.060	0.923	0.000	0.253	0.512

$Q_d=256; f_s=128$

	1	2	3	4	5	6	7	8
a_2	0.018	0.033	0.006	0.001	0.023	0.000	0.031	0.080
a_1	0.209	0.047	0.016	0.027	0.029	0.019	0.189	0.162
a	0.088	0.697	0.364	0.025	0.773	0.000	0.162	0.495

$Q_d=256; f_s=256$)

	1	2	3	4	5	6	7	8
a_2	0.031	0.049	0.015	0.002	0.035	0.000	0.050	0.127
a_1	0.259	0.048	0.006	0.042	0.039	0.025	0.211	0.196
a	0.119	1.028	2.389	0.058	0.908	0.000	0.235	0.648

Next, let's consider the gain and loss for the prefetch policy. Let's define the terms:

- **Prefetch:** Includes post-read and pre-read. Post-read means an additional size is attached to the last LBA; pre-read means an additional size is attached to the first LBA. For example, assume that the original command is to read LBA 10-20 and the pre-read size is 8. Then the extended command is to read LBA 2-20.

- **Gain:** The additional cache hit obtained (b_2) = the cache hit ratio at fetch length x (b_3) - the cache hit ratio without prefetch (b_0)

- **Loss:** The prefetch commands occurs / the total read command (b_1)

- **Gain-loss-ratio $b = b_2/b_1$:** The higher, the better

For this case, let's also consider the number of sequential streams and each stream's length, besides the queue depth and the time interval. The procedure is similar to the previous case. Table 5-13 shows the result. You can see that App 5 is most significant for post-read; while App 6 is less significant. b is generally smaller than 1 for short queue depth. When prefetch size is very small (< 64), b is very small (<< 1). When the queue length and hole length is long, a prefetch policy is generally useful. Based on the value of b, you may say that this policy is generally useless for App 6, most significant for App 5 with post-read, and may be useful for Apps 2, 4, 7, and 8.

Table 5-13. *Gain-Loss Analysis for Prefetch Policy*

$Q_d=128; f_s=128$

	1	2	3	4	5	6	7	8
b_2	0.179	0.140	0.063	0.119	0.462	0.000	0.220	0.224
b_1	0.818	0.859	0.937	0.880	0.528	1.000	0.769	0.764
b	0.219	0.163	0.067	0.136	0.875	0.000	0.286	0.294

$Q_d=128; f_s=256$

	1	2	3	4	5	6	7	8
b_2	0.307	0.417	0.197	0.383	0.607	0.000	0.398	0.321
b_1	0.690	0.582	0.803	0.616	0.382	1.000	0.591	0.668
b	0.444	0.717	0.245	0.621	1.589	0.000	0.674	0.480

$Q_d=256; f_s=128$

	1	2	3	4	5	6	7	8
b_2	0.183	0.147	0.063	0.120	0.461	0.000	0.220	0.239
b_1	0.814	0.851	0.937	0.879	0.527	1.000	0.769	0.748
b	0.225	0.173	0.067	0.137	0.875	0.000	0.286	0.319

$Q_d=256; f_s=256$

	1	2	3	4	5	6	7	8
b_2	0.310	0.427	0.197	0.384	0.607	0.000	0.398	0.342
b_1	0.687	0.572	0.803	0.615	0.381	1.000	0.591	0.645
b	0.452	0.746	0.245	0.625	1.593	0.000	0.674	0.530

You may also analyze the relationship between post-read and sequential stream by counting 1) the stream numbers (c) and the ratio $c_1 = c$/total read numbers; 2) each streams hit frequency c_2; 3) the cache hit as b_2 (only consider post read, redefine b_2). This test can help to check if the infinity sequence read takes effect, such as only when the sequence length is long enough, the cache enters into infinity mode. In infinity mode, post-read is automatic. However, if it is not in infinity mode, you still need to consider the benefit of the post-read, after detecting a two-command sequential stream, like the possibility of three or more commands attached to the stream.

You can further find the relation between prefetch and hole filling by defining

- **Gain:** The additional cache hit obtained (d_2) = the cache hit ratio at fetch length x and hole length y (d_3) - the cache hit ratio without prefetch and hole filling (d_0)

- **Loss:** The additional commands occurs / the total read command (d_1)

- **Gain-loss-ratio $d = d_2/d_1$:** The higher, the better

Two comparison methods are conducted here:

- Two queues, one for prefetch (Q_1) and other for hole filling (Q_2), both under LRU. Consider the overlapped hit ratio, i.e., if a command hits in Q_1, it also hits in Q_2 and vice versa.

- Two queues, one for prefetch (Q_1) and other for hole filling + prefetch (Q_3); both under LRU. Consider the additional hit ratio of Q_3 over Q_1.

Define x_0 as the hit number without prefetch and hole filling policies, $\bar{x}_1 = x_1 + x_0$ as the hit with prefetch, $\bar{x}_2 = x_2 + x_0$ as the hit due to hole filling, and $\bar{x}_3$ as the hit due to combined prefetch and hole filling. Now if x_0 is much larger than x_1 and x_2, it shows that there is not much difference between prefetch and hole filling; otherwise, check the difference between x_1 and x_2. If x_1 is much larger than x_2, it shows that the benefit of fetch is much larger than hole filling; otherwise, it is reasonable to do hole filling instead of prefetch. If $x_3 - x_0$ is much larger than x_1, it indicates that the hole filling gained benefits from refetch; otherwise, prefetch is not beneficial.

Without post-read fetch, you can observe that $\bar{x}_1$ is generally higher than $\bar{x}_2$, and x_1 and x_0 are generally larger than x_2. Except for Apps 5 and 6, x_2 is generally smaller than 1% (Apps 4 and 8 are around 1% when queue length and fetch size are 256). This means that if post-read takes effect, then the hole filling's influence is very small. The overlap between two policies (post only) are much higher than x_1 and $x_1 + x_2$; $x_0/(x_1 + x_2)$ is generally larger than 10 when prefetch size is over 128 (various prefetch size; fixed hole filling size 256). Now the key problem is whether it is worthy to do the hole filling for the additional 2% (queue length =128, fetch size =256/128) cache hit ratio at the cost of additional self-induced access (~ 10%).

Observe that b_1 is generally larger than a_1. However, the cost of each prefetch is generally smaller than that of a self-induced hole filling command. Note that this direct comparison may be unfair. An indirect method is to estimate the average service time for the prefetch policy and hole filling policy (WCD), so for prefetch, define the response time as write ratio *write access time + read ratio *(b_3 *cache access time + $(1-b_3)$* read access time), and for hole filling, define the response time as write ratio *write access time + read ratio *(a_3 *cache access time + $(1-a_3)$* read access time). However, I omit the details here.

In sum, you can see that hole filling policy can improve the cache ratio by introducing self-induced background filling commands.

- The benefit (increased hit frequency) and the cost (additional self-induced commands) ratio of (post) hole filling is generally less than 1 if filling any hole within a certain distance; the average is 0.47 (queue depth = 256; hole size = 256 blks).

- The benefit and the cost ratio of prefetch (post-read) is generally less than 1 if prefetching any non-hit command with a certain prefetch size; the average is 0.68 (queue depth = 256; prefetch size = 256 blks), which is better than a (post) hole filling policy, considering that some hole filling commands may need more recourses than prefetch commands.

- If further applying (post) hole filling policy to the prefetch policy, the additional benefit/cost ratio is generally less than 0.2 (queue depth = 256; prefetch size = 256 blks, hole size = 256 blks). Unless a well-designed hole filling policy (e.g., based on data-correlation) is applied, it is not very useful for overall performance improvement.

Due to the similarity of hole filling and prefetch, the data-correlation methods may be applied to both hole filling and prefetch; thus the two policies might be merged.

CHAPTER 6

Case Study: Modern Disks

Modern disks implement many different features, such as media-based cache (e.g., using a portion of disk space to log some random write accesses), DRAM protection (e.g., using a small-size NVM to temporarily store some data in DRAM cache during a power loss such that write-cache can be always enabled), hybrid structure (e.g., migrating hot data to high-speed devices and cold data to low-speed devices so that the overall access time is reduced), etc. A hybrid disk (e.g., SSHD), one of the hybrid structures, has advantages in some scenarios where data hotness is significant. Some emerging and future techniques like SMR, HAMR, and BPR favor sequential access in order to diminish garbage collection, reduce energy consumption, and/or improve the device life. This chapter shows how trace analysis can help to identify these mechanisms via workload property analysis using two examples: SSHD and SMR drives.

SSHD

In this section, let's explore the mystery behind SSHD's performance enhancement in SPC-1C [53] under WCD: SSD/DRAM cache and the self-learning algorithm [56, 57, 16]. I collected data from the XGIG bus analyzer and monitored the response from LeCroy Scope, with a workload generated by the SPC-1C tool. Some techniques, such as pattern recognition, curve fitting, and queue theory, are applied for analysis.

From Figure 6-1, you can see that the IOPS jumps to two times the traditional HDDs for WCD, so the IOPS of SSHD is around 570, while the traditional HDDs (two models: one is Savvio from Seagate, and the other is Sirius from WD) can only reach around 200 IOPS when the response time is less than or equal to 30ms. The task here is to find the reasons for the performance improvement of hybrid structure via trace analysis. The basic idea is to compare several drives with a certain level of similarity: to inject the same workloads to the similar drives, isolate the similarity, and compare the differences. For example, similar CMR models are selected in Table 6-1.

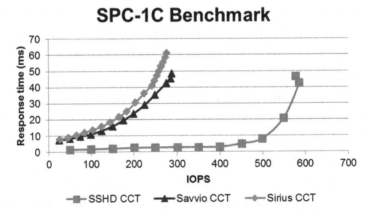

Figure 6-1. *SSHD performance comparison with traditional HDDs*

Table 6-1. *Similar Models Chosen for Comparison*

	SSHD	CMR A	CMR B	CMR C
Capacity (GB)	600	900	600	900
RPM	10.5K	10.5K	10K	10.5K
Bytes per sector	512, 520, 524, 528	512	512	512
Discs	2	3	2	3
Average latency (ms)	2.9	2.9	3	2.9
DRAM cache	128MB	64MB	32MB	64MB
NAND	16GB eMLC	None	None	None
Interface	6Gbps SAS	6Gb/s SAS	6Gb/s SAS	6Gb/s SAS

You know from the previous chapter that the write (random) access dominates the IO requests in SPC-1C, which means the write cache actually plays an important role. However, write cache is supposed to be disabled for WCD. Is it true for this SSHD? To verify it, you can do a simple test by injecting random write requests to SSHD and calculating the CCT/qCCT/TtoD time. If write cache is actually disabled, all requests will be written to media directly, which cost roughly 10ms response time. However, from the trace, you can observe that there are many requests with response times of less than 1ms at the beginning. Therefore, write cache actually is active even for the WCD setting. This benefits from the technique of NAND-backed DRAM cache protection, so part of cached data can be written to NAND just after system power loses.

Now let's start some analysis for two essential problems: the cache size and access isolation.

Cache Size

We begin with the question of *"how much DRAM is used as write cache during WCD?"* First, let's make sure that the test is repeatable (or the result is consistent). In order to verify this, perform the following procedure.

1. Connect SSHD to the XGIG bus analyzer and power off/on SSHD.

2. Send 100 random write 8K requests to SSHD using IOMeter or another tool, and repeat the same requests 10 times.

3. Repeat Steps 1-2 for 4 times with the same requests.

4. Compare and find the access pattern for the XGIG traces via a trace analyzer tool.

5. Repeat Steps 1-4 with the request number changed to 200 and 400.

6. Do the same test on a different SSHD with the same IO pattern.

In Step 4, a similar access pattern (LBA vs. CCT) should be observed. Note that you are checking DRAM write cache in this case, so only a random write request is used. For a full cache check, you may also try random read, mixed read/write, and mixed random/sequential patterns. If a similar pattern is observed, you may conclude that the result is consistent and useful to identify some inside information. Otherwise, you shall find out the reasons. One is that the SSD/DRAM cache is not cleaned before a new test. Therefore, you need some cache flush commands or disk initialization commands to force it empty. Also note that:

- R/W DRAM cache may share the same space.

- The SSD mapping table may share the same space with R/W DRAM cache (a good case: SSD mapping table uses a dedicated DRAM space).

- The SSD reboot self-learning procedure may take DRAM space.

Second, implement the following procedure to make sure each test starts with a clean cache:

1. Power off/on SSHD (make sure the DRAM write cache is cleared).

2. Send 1000 random 8K write requests to SSHD with queue depth=1 using IOMeter.

3. Repeat Steps 1-2 for 10 times each with different request sizes, such as 16K, 32K, 64K, 128K, ..., 2048K.

Once you capture the traces, some post-processes shall be made:

1. Count the write DRAM hit number at the first portion of the total accesses for each run by isolating DRAM accesses from others (DRAM CCT/qCCT is generally much smaller than others).

2. Choose the maximum number of each count.

3. Calculate the hit numbers and the corresponding actual cache size.

4. Find the turning point, which provides a hint of the cluster size.

5. Refine the turning point by narrowing the region. For example, if the turning point is within [256K-512K], then some more points, such as 300K, 400K, and 500K, may be used.

147

Note that this model of SSHD has read-cache only SSD so that DRAM access will not be mixed with SSD write access, which simplifies the analysis in Figures 6-2-6-5. Figure 6-2 shows the traces from IOmeter random write tests (request size from 1K to 1M). Assume that the write cache is empty.[1] Then the first portion of each run could be the DRAM write cache hit.

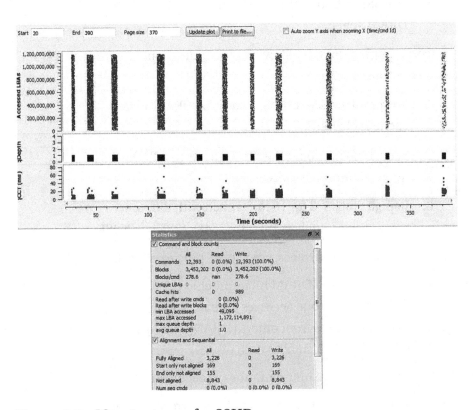

Figure 6-2. *IOmeter traces for SSHD*

---

[1]Even if you follow the instruction here to clean the DRAM, it may not completely true; thus you can also judge it by the fact that no seek is heard.

Zoom into the system to find out the hit. Figures 6-3, 6-4, and 6-5 give three examples where the request sizes are 1KB, 512KB, and 1MB, respectively. In Figures 6-3 and 6-4, you can observe obvious write cache hits, and the total hit number for 1KB is much larger than that of 512KB due to limited cache size. However, when the size is increased to 1MB, no obvious write cache is observed, or it means that one threshold between 512K and 1M is set as the turning point for different size requests. This also indicates that large size requests will go directly to the media. With the same steps, you can actually get the required values for WCD and WCE, as shown in Tables 6-2 and 6-3.

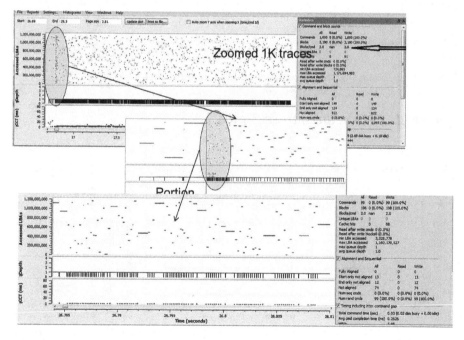

Figure 6-3. *1K request trace details*

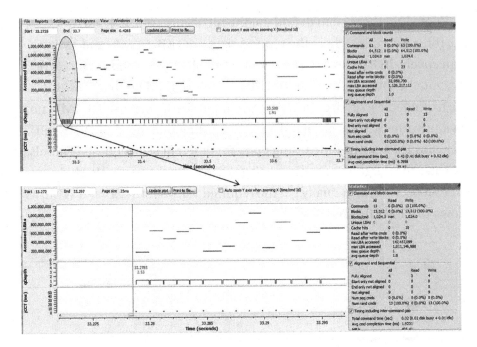

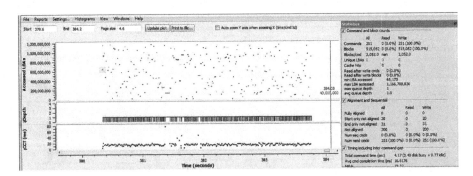

Figure 6-4. *512K request trace details*

Figure 6-5. *1024K request trace details*

Table 6-2. *Comparison Under WCE*

SSHD			CMR A			
Size	Counted number	Size	Size	Counted number	Size	
1K	98	0.1M	1K	98	0.1M	
4k	98	0.4M	4k	98	0.4M	
16K	97	1.5M	16K	99	1.5M	
64K	102	6.4M	64K	102	6.4M	2
128K	103	12.9M	128K	104	12.9M	
256K	111	27.8M	256K	110	27.8M	
512K	115	57.5M	512K	66	33M	
520K	-	-	880K	35	30M	
900K	-	-	900K	42	36.9M	
1024K	N.A.	-	1000K	36	36M	

Table 6-3. *Two Cases Under WCD of SSHD*

SSHD (WCD)	test1		test2	
size	Counted number	Size	Counted number	Size
1K	98	0.1M	101	101K
4k	100	0.4M	100	400K
16K	99	1.5K	100	1600K
64K	101	6.3K	101	6464K
128K	54	6.75M	54	6.75M
256K	26	6.5M	26	6.5M
512K	12	6.0M	13	6.5M
520K	-	-	12	6.1M

From the turning point, you may also guess the cache cluster/segment size. For example, SSHD's cluster size is around 64K for write during WCD, and CMR A is around 256KB. SSHD uses up to 60MB DRAM space as write cache when WCE, while only around 8MB is used for WCD with some 100 segments.

Access Isolation

You saw in the previous chapter that SPC-1C has a large portion of local accesses. This property brings the possibility that some data can be cached into DRAM or SSD and be accessed quickly later. Then the second question is "*how many accesses are actually directed to DRAM or SSD?*" It is generally a difficult task. However, as the access times of DRAM, SSD, and HDD are significantly different, you may isolate the possible commands in different places roughly. The basic idea is to observe the behaviors of the different accesses and then apply data classification and pattern recognition methods to find the access pattern, and do repeated random read tests to finally find the turning points. Although the procedure is similar to the previous case, you need to change the number of requests to SSHD in this case:

1. Send 100/200/256/257/etc. pieces of 8K requests to SSHD, repeat 20-100 times for each number, and refine the number of commands to be sent according to the access pattern.

2. Suppose the turn point is X. Send X random read commands with size 16K,32K,..., and 1024K to SSHD and find the cluster size according to the turning point.

To verify if the repeat number is high enough, check the steady states of response time. Figure 6-6 provides an example where 100 rounds are run. You can see that since the third round, the average value and standard derivatives of response times are almost constant. Thus 10 times of repeats should be enough in this case.

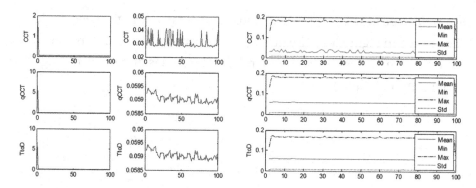

Figure 6-6. *Steady state of response time*

Figure 6-7 shows a case where 100 random read requests with 8KB size were sent to SSHD 20 times. In the first round, all reads went to media. After several rounds, the read requests become hot and eventually all cached in DRAM. Slowly increase the number of requests to check how many requests the DRAM read cache can hold.

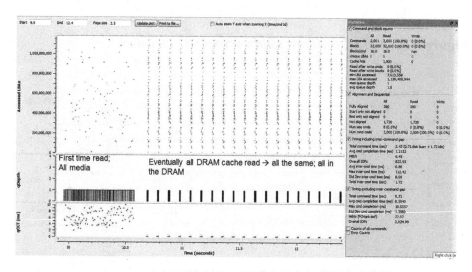

Figure 6-7. *100 8K random reads, repeated 20 times*

Figure 6-8 illustrates the results for 250 requests repeatedly. You can see that DRAM cache can fully hold at least 250 segments. However, when you slightly increase it to 257, destage starts. When further increase to 260,

DRAM destage to SSD happens obviously at a relatively high speed, which is illustrated in Figure 6-9. The destage has a certain adaptive steps, so when the hit number (access frequency) of the data is increased, destage becomes more frequent.

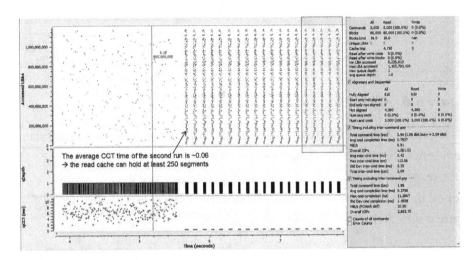

Figure 6-8. *250 8K random reads, repeated 100 times*

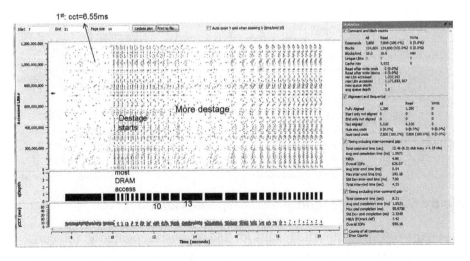

Figure 6-9. *260 8K random reads, repeated 100 times*

Thus, you may guess that 256 could be the maximum read segment number, as no destage happens if this maximum segment number is not exceeded. Note that you can find the destage pattern via different time intervals and sizes.

I leave an issue on request access identification on devices here. Take a look at Figure 6-10, where repeated 260 8KB read requests were sent to SSHD 100 times. As the number is over DRAM's capacity, some requests will go to SSD. The response time of the 1st, 3rd, 14th, 20th and 50th runs is shown. You can see that the very first run all went to disk. Starting at the second round, some went to DRAM and some to media. In the 20th round, the accesses to DRAM, SSD, and media all existed. However, around 50 rounds, most requests went to DRAM and SSD. In fact, you can see a clear gap of response time for these read requests. Basically, you may say that those below 0.1ms are DRAM accesses, and those above 0.2ms are most from SSD. Now you can get the statistical values for the response time of SSD and DRAM in an estimated sense, as shown in Table 6-4.

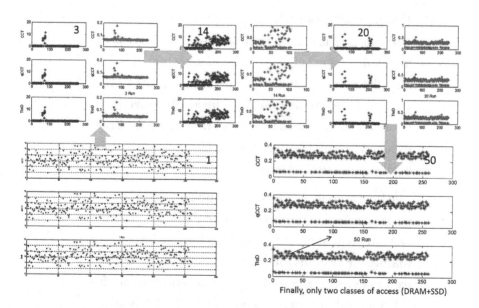

Figure 6-10. *Read response time pattern over repeated rounds*

Table 6-4. *Statistics on Response Time (Based on 40-90 Rounds)*

260	Average	CCT	qCCT	TtoD
Overall	Mean	0.227	0.227	0.212
	Std.	0.096	0.096	0.096
SSD	Mean	0.279	0.279	0.264
	Std.	0.031	0.031	0.032
DRAM	Mean	0.063	0.063	0.048
	Std.	0.001	0.001	0.001

SMR

This section will discuss the main characteristics of SMR [4, 5] and the interaction between these characteristics and particular workloads. The industry has two approaches for SMR generally:

- The drive manages all data accesses, and data management is complicated similar to the FTL (flash translation layer) of SSD, so the management of metadata, GC (garbage collection), over-provisioning, variable performance, etc, is all inside the drive. However, there are no host-side changes, so the drive is used as a normal one. Currently, all major SMR drives available in the market fall in this category.

- The host manages most data-related accesses via a SMR-specific file system similar to flash file system. Data management is complicated but can leverage mature file systems that write sequentially. A few examples are SFS [58], HiSMRfs [59], and Shingledfs [5]. Although mixed drive-host management is also possible, it is really rare.

156

Many particular design issues are considered for SMR drives, such as data layout management (layout, data placement, defragmentation, GC, pointer to bands), mixed zones (combine shingled and unshingled part in same disk), SMR algorithms, and structure for specific applications, etc. Table 6-5 lists some main expected workload characteristics for SMR so that those applications with designed metrics can work perfectly in SMR drives.

Table 6-5. *SMR Characteristics vs. Workload Metrics*

SMR char	SMR expectation	Workload metrics	SMR impact
Sequential write	Good for large size sequential write requests	Average write request size and distribution Seek distance (LBA) Sequential stream and near-sequential stream	The larger size, the better The smaller seek distance, the more sequential The more streams, the more sequential
Write once read-many	Good for less updates and more reads	Read/write ratio Read on write (ROW) hit ratio Write update ratio	The higher read/write ratio (ROW ratio), the better The smaller the write update ratio, the better
Garbage collection (GC)	Smaller write amplification and less GC	Device utilization, device idle time distribution, queue length IOPS, throughput Frequented/timed/ stacked write update ratio (WUR) Write on write (WOW) hit distribution and ratio	Long and frequent idle time for GC Low write update ratio indicates that less GC is required

(continued)

Table 6-5. (*continued*)

SMR char	SMR expectation	Workload metrics	SMR impact
Sequential read to random write	Less read performance impact due to indirect mapping, such as sequential LBA read requests in random physical address	Read on write (ROW) hit/size distribution and ratio	The higher the small (large) read to small (large) write ratio, the better
In-place or out-of-place update	Frequent and recent updates need random access zone (RAZ)/SSD/ large DRAM buffer to hold write data	Stacked write update ratio	The higher ratio in shorter stack, the more necessary to have an in-place update buffer

CHAPTER 7

Case Study: RAID

RAID is one of the most widely applied data-protection strategies in the world [23, 60, 61, 62, 63]. It has unique features compared with single disk access, such as file synchronization, recovery, etc. Therefore, it leads to some unique IO patterns compared with others. This chapter analyzes two examples based on RAID 5 from two application scenarios. Large differences are observed between two traces. This chapter also analyzes whether the workloads are suitable for SMR drives. In addition, some suggestions are provided in order to improve system performance.

The concept of a RAID was introduced to harness the potential of commodity hard drives in 1987. Patterson et al. [64] officially established the RAID taxonomy in 1988. RAID overcomes the capacity limitations of commodity disks by exposing an array of such low-capacity disks as a virtual single large expensive disks (SLED).

RAID technology usually requires the distribution of data across a number of disks via the data stripes. A stripe represents the smallest unit of protection in an array, thus any lost data within a stripe can be recovered using only the surviving data within that stripe. In early days, since clients were connected to the RAID via a serial access channel, parallel access by multiple clients was not explicitly supported. However, with many advanced queuing schedulers developed, parallelism now is widely applied in RAID systems in order to fully utilize the advantage of multiple disks.

© Jun Xu 2018
J. Xu, *Block Trace Analysis and Storage System Optimization*,
https://doi.org/10.1007/978-1-4842-3928-5_7

There are some common performance issues within RAID systems [20, 62, 63], such as the small write problem, the synchronization problem, performance loss during downgrade (recovery and reconstruction), and more.

The small write problem exists in many critical applications, such as online transaction processing (OLTP) systems. Those applications usually contain many read-modify-write (RMW) accesses. This leads to some issues for a RAID system. First, a write in a striped array requires reads of both data and parity blocks, and computation of a new parity, before the writing of both new data and new parity, which is four times more accesses than for a single disk. Second, these small accesses only alter a few blocks within a specific stripe, yet the parity disk for the entire stripe is unavailable during the update. This dramatically downgrades the performance of the array by reducing the possible parallelism.

The synchronization problem is due to the data integrity requirements; only when all drives of one stripe array are completed, the system returns a completion signal. Since some disks may finish access earlier than others, the faster disks have to wait for the slow ones. This requirement may be relieved in some conditions, such as non-critical applications, protected DRAM, etc. During recovery, due to background recovery access, the foreground user requests may be largely impacted [65].

Similar problems are also applicable to the disk arrays using erasure code (EC). And in some cases, the problem may be more critical due to the higher complexity of EC than that of traditional RAID.

Workload Analysis

You will study two RAID 5 examples from two different vendors under video surveillance applications. The system settings will be given first, followed by the analysis of two different traces: read-dominant and write-dominant cases.

System Settings

In the first example, there are 10 7200RPM HDDs each of 4TB. 24 write streams and 6 read streams are imposed to this system. The second example has 36 similar HDDs with 90 video channels. The trace length is 620 and 110 seconds, respectively. Some basic metrics are listed in Tables 7-1 and 7-2.

Table 7-1. *RAID Trace 1: Read Dominated*

	Combined	Read	Write
Numbers of commands	7821	5493 (70.2%)	2328 (29.8%)
Number of blocks	5284520	3231312 (61.1%)	2053208 (38.9%)
Average size (block)	675.7	588.3	882

r/s	w/s	rsec/s	wsec/s	rkB/s	wkB/s	IOPS	TP(MBPS)
8.86	3.75	5211.8	3311.6	2605.9	1655.8	12.61	4.23

Table 7-2. *RAID Trace 2: Write Dominated*

Metrics	Combined	Read	Write
Cmd number	21449	8535	12914
Total blk size	2528514	357824	2170690
Average blk size	210.012	41.924	168.088
Average IOPS	193.152	76.859	116.293
Average TP (MBps)	11.118	1.573	9.545

Read-Dominated Trace

The LBA distribution of requests are near sequential in this trace, as shown in Figure 7-1. For reads, there are two regions. One is the same to the current write region, and the other is close to the previous write region (i.e., playback). The sizes of the read requests are mostly 512 or 1024 blocks. However, the ratio of 1024 blocks of read is less than that of write, which is displayed in Figure 7-2.

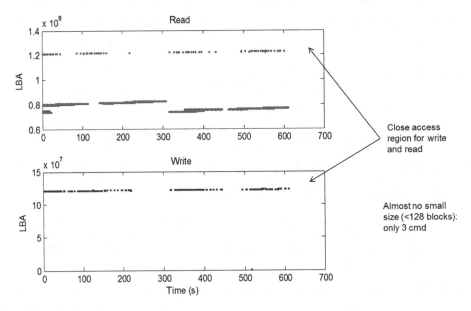

Figure 7-1. *LBA distribution of RAID Trace 1*

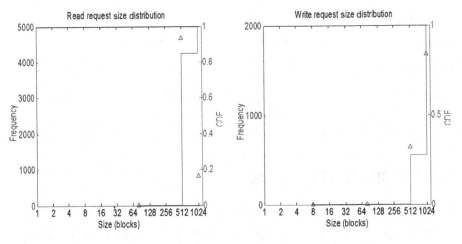

Figure 7-2. *Size distribution of RAID trace 1*

In general, this trace has large portion of idle time, which accumulates 83.4% of total time. The average summation of idle time is almost evenly distributed over time but the large idle intervals not, as shown in Figure 7-3. The intervals >200ms and >500ms count 8% and 1.7%, respectively, but occupy 71.6% and 34% of total idle time, respectively. In fact, 65% (94%) of idle frequency is less than 10ms (1s), and 2% (70%) of idle time is less than 10ms (1s), as illustrated in Figure 7-4. So we can conclude that the total idle time is long enough for small-IO-based background activities, but the individual long idle intervals may be not sufficient, which means GC access shall be completed in small steps.

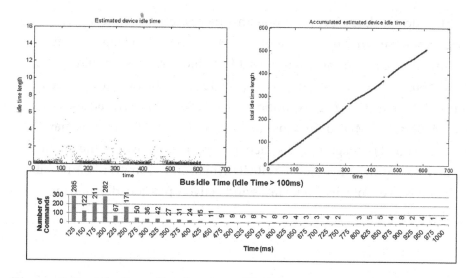

Figure 7-3. *Idle time distribution of RAID trace 1*

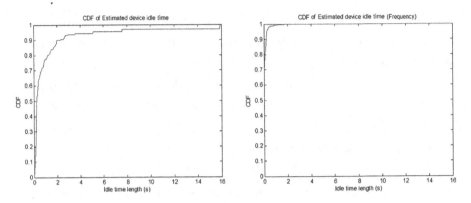

Figure 7-4. *Idle time CDF of RAID trace 1*

Besides the large idle time, note that there are some abnormally large response times for some requests (> 200*ms*). As you know, even for the worst case, the access time of a 1024-block request should not excess 60ms. Thus, the waiting time is too long for the two cases listed in Table 7-3: 1) the CMD 529 is continuous to 530 but the write access costs over 430ms; 2) CMD 1015 is close to 1024 but it costs 390ms. This may be caused by 1) background disk activities such as log writes, metadata updates, zone switches, etc; or 2) RAID synchronization events. A possible solution is to evenly distribute tasks and actively provide idle time for background tasks.

Table 7-3. *A Segment of RAID Trace 1*

Start(sec)	End	ID	End	Cmd	ICT(ms)	LBA	Length
27.51865	27.53302	529	529	W	0.109105	1.21e+08	1024
27.5331	27.96851	530	530	W	0.078425	1.21e+08	512
27.9686	27.98473	531	531	R	0.086485	80135168	1024
27.98483	27.987	532	532	R	0.10257	80351232	512
...							
52.73206	52.7429	1014	1014	R	0.466475	80690688	512
53.46918	53.85766	1015	1015	R	726.2745	80875520	512
53.85778	53.86006	1016	1016	R	0.112894	80876032	512
53.86014	53.87545	1017	1017	R	0.083455	80881664	1024

For the frequented write update shown in Figure 7-5, you can see that 94.2% of the accessed blocks (maybe repeated) are only written once and 5.8% of the blocks are at least accessed twice and <0.1% of the blocks are written three times. This means a very low rewritten ratio. Thus you need to identify if large size requests or small size requests are rewritten most. The fact that decreasing percentage of written blocks are written multiple times means a tiny portion of hot blocks.

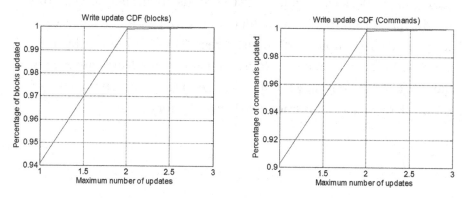

Figure 7-5. *Frequented update of RAID trace 1*

For the timed write update shown in Figure 7-6, the total write blocks occurs 35% of total access blocks (read and write) and the updated blocks (at least write twice) are only 1% (1/35=2.9% rewritten blocks). Total write commands are 30% of the total commands and the update commands are 1.5%. Note that the timed write update ratio is closely related to the frequented write update ratio; in other words, sum(hit*(update freq-1))/ total blocks = updated blocks/total write blocks.

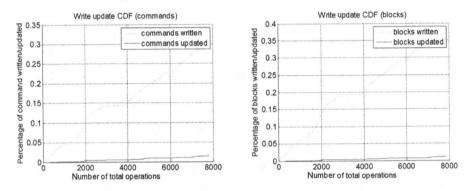

Figure 7-6. *Timed update of RAID trace 1*

By further considering the write stack distance in Figure 7-7, you can see that the hit ratio is low and it is not necessary to have an inline write cache to hold these write data for a long time. Based on IOPS, to reach stack distance 100, it costs roughly 26.6 seconds. In this period, only 10% full write hit and 20% partial write hit of the overall 5% hit are observed. The updated size is around 43MB on average. Thus it is not worthy of compensating such a small hit. Note that the write hit distributes over the write range. A full hit is only for 512-block requests while a partial hit is for 1024-block requests in this trace. See Figure 7-8 for details.

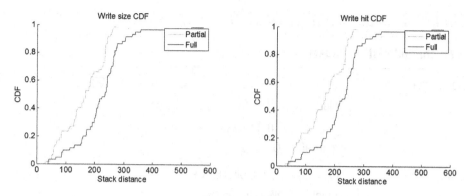

Figure 7-7. *Stack update of RAID trace 1*

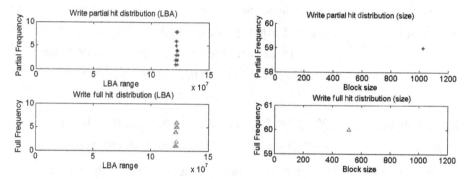

Figure 7-8. *Write hit distribution of RAID trace 1*

When you take SMR drive into consideration, as discussed in Chapter 6, you have the main characteristics summarized in Table 7-4. You may understand this table together with the SMR properties introduced in Chapter 6. Although it is a read-dominated trace, it has no WORM property.

Table 7-4. *Main Characteristics of Trace 1 for SMR*

SMR characteristic	Observation
Sequential write	Large size write requests *(>=512 blocks)* > 99.9% Mode ratio: 50% for read & write (Q=1) Sequential cmd ratio(M>=2 & S>=1024): write 85% & read 90% (Q>=50)
Write-once-read-many	R/W: cmd 70:30; blks 61:39 Stacked ROW ratio: < 1% Total write blocks occurs 2.9% of total access blocks
Garbage collection (GC)	Frequent small idle time; short queue length 5.8% frequented WUR the updated blocks (at least write twice) are only 1% of total access blocks and 2.9% write blocks, so very small write update ratio and write amplification 103% (considering the short trace duration)
Sequential read to random write	ROW ratio is 1.2, so it's a very small read ratio, thus the written data is rarely likely to be immediately read back
In-place or out-of-place update	Very small update ratio; not necessary to apply large-size SSD/DRAM/AZR cache for performance improvement (write update in cache)

Write-Dominated Trace

This trace from a video surveillance application shows a large difference from the previous one in many aspects, such as the read/write ratio, LBA distribution, size distribution, write update ratio, etc. Therefore, for different venders under different scenarios, the actual workloads may differ from each other significantly, even using the same storage structure.

Figure 7-9 shows the LBA distribution where only one main region spanning 30GB is applied to both read and write close to the starting position of LBA (as the trace was collected when the RAID is nearly empty).

If you further consider the figure of LBA vs. Time, you can see that the write requests are more sequential than the read ones. Figure 7-10 illustrates that write and read have similar size distribution, dominated 8-block requests, and close shape of 8-128 blocks distribution. Also, the size distribution range is much larger than the previous trace.

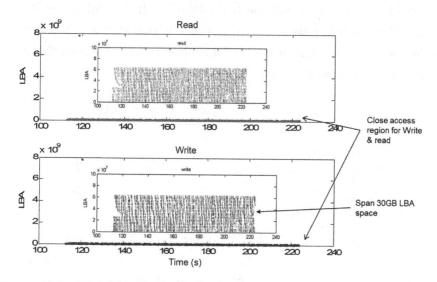

Figure 7-9. *LBA distribution of RAID trace 2*

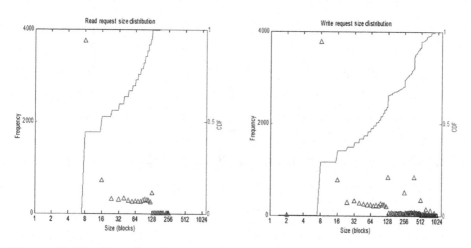

Figure 7-10. *Size distribution of RAID trace 2*

As it is write dominated, let's focus more on the write update. Figure 7-11 shows the stacked distance for write requests. This confirms the timed write update, which is the small overlap size (possibly due to metadata block attached to data blocks). From Figure 7-12, the stack distance 250 is roughly 2.1 seconds based on IOPS. In this period, it's near 60% full write hit and 60% partial write hit of the overall 52% write command hit. This means that some portions kept updating. Therefore, the disk or system may require a random access zone or NVM for this small portion of updated data.

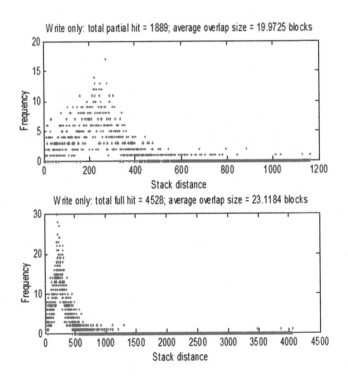

Figure 7-11. *Write stack distance of RAID trace 2*

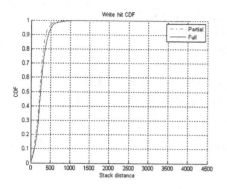
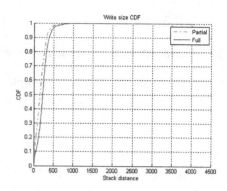

Figure 7-12. *Stack update of RAID trace 2*

In sum, tens of mixed streams lead to a not-very-sequential IO pattern, which indicates that a proper stream-detection algorithm with long queue is required. Special metadata and parity structure lead to a relatively high LBA update size and large update command ratio, which implies that a large size DRAM/NVM/RAZ cache may be necessary to avoid the frequent updates. Also, you can conclude that the impact of write cache is very limited in the previous read-dominated trace. Note the frequent small idles but less effective idle intervals, which indicates that GC policy may be adjusted to fit this situation.

The impact to SMR drives is summarized in Table 7-5. Essentially, the impact for normal write access is not trivial due to the relatively large update ratio. The high updated command ratio may cause relative high defragmentation. The metadata management scheme of the surveillance system and/or the SMR drives may require changes. The drive may not have enough idle time for the background GC subject to GC policy, as the useful effective idle intervals are marginal.

Table 7-5. *Main Characteristics of Trace 2 wrt SMR*

SMR characteristics	Hadoop observation
Sequential write	Large size write requests (>=128 blocks): 35% Mode ratio: 18% (27%) for write when Q=1(Q=128) Sequential cmd ratio(M>=2): write 35% at QL=1 & 60% at Q=256
Write-once-read-many	R/W: cmd 1:1.5; blks 1:6.1 High stacked ROW ratio Total write blocks occurs 85.9% of total access blocks
Garbage collection (GC)	Updated blocks (at least write twice) are 13.4% of write blocks, so a relatively high write update ratio and write amplification 115.5% (considering the short trace duration) Updated command ratio >50% with small overlap possibly due to the metadata attached Frequent but small-size idle time in host side difficult for background GC
In-place or out-of-place update	Relatively high update ratio, so it's necessary to apply large-size SSD/DRAM/AZR cache for performance improvement (write update in cache)

This trace is much busier than the previous one. The total effective idle time (idle interval>0.1s) is 14.40 seconds and total idle time 98.6 seconds. The total effective idle frequency (idle interval>0.1s) is 33 only while the total idle frequency is 6244. Now the question is whether the (effective) idle time is enough for background activities. Due to the relatively consistent workload of video surveillance and data/metadata structure, the garbage ratio of each SMR data zone is similar. Suppose a 1GB for zone size and 3MB per track. The total write workload of this trace is about 1GB. So is it possible to move 1GB to new place in the effective idle times? Here is the analysis:

- Completion of a sequential 1GB read and a sequential 887MB write (assume13.4% garbage ratio) requires around 5.3 seconds for 7200RPM.

- The average useful idle time for GC is 14.4/33–0.1=0.34 second. Suppose the positioning time is 6ms for R/W. (0.34–0.006*2) second can handle up to 64.4MB data in GC zone.[1] A total of 33 idle intervals can handle around 2GB data, which is larger than 1GB.

- Additionally, the old video data is replaced by new data periodically, which will not change the garbage ratio much in general.

Ideally, the idle time seems large enough to handle GC activities, given that

- The effective idle time should be fully used and the GC size is adjusted dynamically.

- The idle time algorithm works quite well with a lower idle detection threshold, such as from 100ms to 50ms to increase the GC activities.

- The other background activities may not take much time.

However, in reality, you may require much large idle time. In particular, defragmentation may significantly increase the write amplification ratio.

---

[1]"This can be solved by the following optimization problem: $\max$ cleaned_ data=read_speed*$t1\_$+write_speed*t_2, subject to t_1+t_2=0.34–0.006*2 and t_1, t_2>0".

CHAPTER 8

Case Study: Hadoop

Hadoop is one of the most popular distributed big data platforms in the world. Besides computing power, its storage subsystem capability is also a key factor in its overall performance. In particular, there are many intermediate file exchanges for MapReduce. This chapter presents the block-level workload characteristics of a Hadoop cluster by considering some specific metrics. The analysis techniques presented can help you understand the performance and drive characteristics of Hadoop in production environments. In addition, this chapter also identifies whether SMR drives are suitable for the Hadoop workload.

Users of large systems must deal with explosive data generation, often from a multitude of different sources and formats. The observation and extraction of potential value contained in this large, generally unstructured data lead to great challenges, but also opportunities in data storage, management, and processing. From a data storage perspective, huge capacity (byte) growth is expected, with HDDs supplying most capacity workloads for the foreseeable future, although SSDs and NVMs are also widely used in time-sensitive scenarios (performance workload). The interaction of HDDs with these capacity workloads must be well understood so that these devices algorithms.

© Jun Xu 2018
J. Xu, *Block Trace Analysis and Storage System Optimization*,
https://doi.org/10.1007/978-1-4842-3928-5_8

From data management and processing, big data arises as a trendy technology, while Hadoop emerges as a leading solution. Originating from Google's GFS and MapReduce framework, the open-source Hadoop has gained much popularity due to its availability, scalability, and good economy of scale. Hadoop's performance has been illustrated for batch MapReduce tasks in many cases [66, 67], though more exploration is ongoing for other applications within Hadoop's umbrella of frameworks.

To best understand Hadoop's performance, a common approach is workload analysis [66, 67, 68, 69, 70]. The workload can be collected and viewed in different abstract levels. The references [37, 35] suggest three classifications: functional, system, and physical (see Figure 2-1 in Chapter 2). However, most workload analysis works in this area are studied with a system view.

Kavulya et al. [71] analyzed 10 months of MapReduce logs from the Yahoo! M45 cluster, applied learning techniques to predict job completion times from historical data, and identified potential performance problems in their dataset. Abda et al. [72] analyzed six-month traces from two large Hadoop clusters at Yahoo! and characterized the file popularity, temporal locality, and arrival patterns of the workloads, while Ren et al. [66] provided MapReduce workload analysis of 2000+ nodes in Taobao's e-commerce production environment. Wang et al. [67] evaluated Hadoop job schedulers and quantified the impact of shared storage on Hadoop system performance, and therefore synthesize realistic cloud workloads. Shafer et al. [70] investigated the root causes of performance bottlenecks in order to evaluate trade-offs between portability and performance in Hadoop via different workloads. Ren et al. [73] analyzed three different Hadoop clusters to explore new issues in application patterns and user behavior and to understand key performance challenges related to IO and load balance. And many other notable examples exist as well [69, 68, 37].

While predominately system-focused, some works provide a functional view [69, 70, 73] where average traffic volume from historical web logs are discussed. Some simulators and synthetic workload generators are also suggested, such as Ankus [66], MRPerf [74], and its enhancement [67].

However, to my best knowledge, there is no direct analysis work for a Hadoop system at the block level. A block-level analysis is timely and more valuable now that device manufacturers are pressured to develop/ improve products to meet capacity or performance demands, such as emerging hybrid or shingled magnetic recording (SMR) drives [5, 40, 4]. When considering the SMR drives (and the coming energy/heat assistant magnetic recording (EAMR/HAMR) drives) which have much higher data density than conventional drives, such an analysis is indispensable, due to their distinguished features from the conventional drives. For example, SMR drives introduce characteristics such as shingled tracks, which make the device more amenable to sequential writes over random, as well as indirect block address mapping, garbage collection, and more, which all modify how these devices interact with user workloads. A big question at the device level is if the block-level Hadoop workload is suitable in SMR drives.

In this chapter, I analyze Hadoop workloads at a block device level and answer this big question. Aided by blktrace, I provide a clear view of Hadoop's behavior in storage devices [75, 76]. The main contribution lies in the following aspects:

- Defining some new block-level workload metrics, such as stacked write update, stacked ROW, and queued seek distance to fulfill particular requirement of disk features

- Identifying some characteristics of a big organization's internal Hadoop cluster, and relating them to findings of other published Hadoop clusters with similarity and difference

- Providing some suggestions on Hadoop performance bolstered from drive-level support

- Providing analysis for the applicability of SMR drives in Hadoop workloads

This chapter will first cover the overall background of SMR drives and the Hadoop cluster and trace collection procedure. Then it will cover the analysis results based on these metrics.

Hadoop Cluster

Numerous workload studies have been conducted at various levels, from the user perspective to system/framework-level analysis. Most of these types of analysis only capture certain characteristics of the system. Harter et al. go as far as to take traces at a system view and apply a simple simulator to provide a physical view of the workload [77]. However, leaving the physical view of a system to simulation can miss details that may be critical to understanding a workload. Therefore, it is generally more reasonable to analyze the real workloads when considering performance.

The workflow of a Hadoop cluster is to import large and unstructured datasets from global manufacturing facilities into the HDFS. Once imported, the data is crunched and then organized into more structured data via MapReduce applications. Finally, this data is given to HBase for real-time analysis of the once previously unstructured data. While some of this structured data is kept on the HDFS (or moved to another storage location), the unstructured data is deleted daily in preparation to receive new manufacturing data.

The Hadoop cluster is used to store the manufacturing information, such as the data from 200 million devices per year created by the company. For example, in phase I manufacturing (clean room assembly), while drive components are assembled, data is captured by various sensors at each construction step for every drive. From a manufacturing point of view, creating 50-60 million devices a quarter creates petabytes of information that must be collected, stored, and disseminated in the organization for different needs. Some user scenarios include the query to the particular models, the summarization of quality of one batch, the average media density of one model, etc.

PIG/Hive is used for MapReduce indirectly, actually PIG/Hive converts SQL-like code to Java code to run MapReduce. MapReduce then does SQL-like statements to process raw test data to generate drill-downs and dashboards for product engineering R&D and failure analysis (FA). However, the cluster is mainly for analytics: MapReduce use cases (~80%) and also some Hbase online search use cases (~20%).

The WD cluster configuration is shown in Table 8-1. A general data flow is shown in Figure 8-1, where HDFS has native configurable logging structure, while datanode needs the aid of blktrace. The read requests from client-obtained metadata information from the namenode and then namenode sends block ops to devices. Thus the client gets the corresponding data from datanotes. The write requests will change both data in datanodes and the metadata in namenodes.

Table 8-1. *WD-HDP1 Cluster Configuration*

WD-HDP1: 100 Servers	
CPU	Intel Xeon E3-1240v2, 4 Core
RAM	32 GB DDR3
OS HDD	WDC WD3000BLFS 10kRPM 300GB
Hadoop HDD	WDC WD2000FYYX 7.2kRPM 2-4TB
Hadoop Version	1.2.x

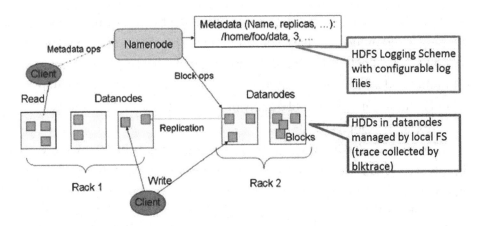

Figure 8-1. *Data flow in Hadoop system*

The data collection structure is illustrated in Figure 8-2. The task tracker runs above the local file system (FS). The jobs will finally convert into the block-level accesses to the local devices in each datanode. The tool blktrace actually collects the data in the block IO layer from the local devices (see Appendix B for details). I ran blktrace (sometimes together with iostat and/or iotop) repeatedly on four datanodes with different file systems and write cache settings in tens of batches, where two nodes used XFS and another two used EXT4 as local file systems, with each run lasting for few hours to few days. I collected hundreds of GB of traces (100+ pieces) representing total 1500+ hours of cluster operation from May 2014 to January 2015.[1] I switched the write cache on or off to collect data from different situations. The workload to these four nodes was relatively stable based on Ganglia's network in/out metrics except for a few pieces. In particular, I focus on the trace collected in January 2015 with batch ID from 16 to 25 in this book. They are all one-day duration traces with the settings as show in Table 8-2.

---

[1]Trace is available up request. Please contact WDLabs for details at https://community.wd.com/c/wdlabs.

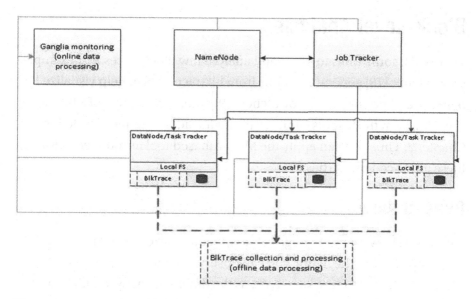

Figure 8-2. *Trace collection using Ganglia and Blktrace*

Table 8-2. *File System and Write Cache Settings*

Node ID	FS	Write cache
147	XFS	16:21 disabled; 22:25 enabled
148	EXT4	16:21 disabled; 22:25 enabled
149	EXT4	16:21 enabled; 22:25 disabled
150	XFS	16:21 enabled; 22:25 disabled

Workload Metrics Evaluation

In this section, I discuss my observations of disk activity from a sample of
nodes within the Hadoop cluster. I then explain how these observations
relate to metrics discussed in the previous section. Finally, I conclude
with observations from a system level and suggestions for addressing
performance issues which could arise from my recorded observations.

Block-Level Analysis

There exist some tools to parse and analyze raw block traces. For example, seekwatcher [78] generates graphs from blktrace runs to help visualize IO patterns and performance. Iowatcher [79] graphs the results of a blktrace run. However, those tools cannot capture the advanced metrics defined in Chapter 2. Thus you can apply the Matlab-based tool introduced before for these advanced properties.

General View

Figure 8-3 shows some average values of request size, IOPS, and throughput. From the figure, you can observe that the write size and IOPS are more related to file system type, as the difference between EXT4 and XFS is obvious. However, the read size and IOPS seem to be more related to batch, as different batches may have different read sizes. Note that the overall throughput is similar for each batch, which means the workload to each node is nearly even.[2] By removing the maximum and minimum values, you can look at the average value and standard derivatives in Figure 8-4. The size pattern for write for different file system types is clearly illustrated. Figure 8-5 further shows that the write requests' major size range is [1–127] blocks and 1024 blocks. The sum of ratios in the two ranges is almost equal to 1, which leads to the near symmetric curve around 0.475.

---

[2]There may exist a few nodes with large variance compared with others due to non-perfect workload balance policy.

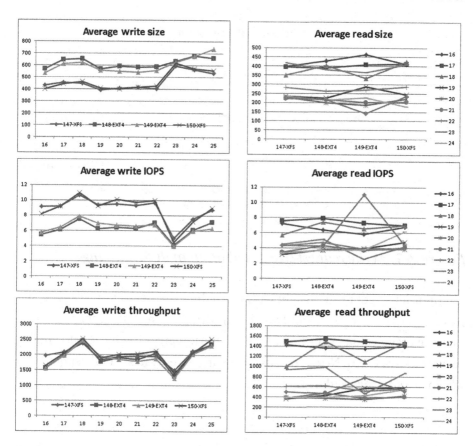

Figure 8-3. *Average values of workloads for different file systems*

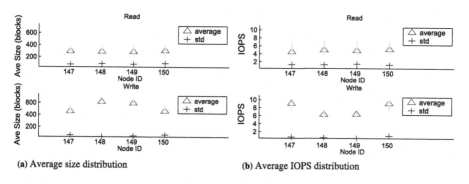

(a) Average size distribution

(b) Average IOPS distribution

Figure 8-4. *Average size and IOPS*

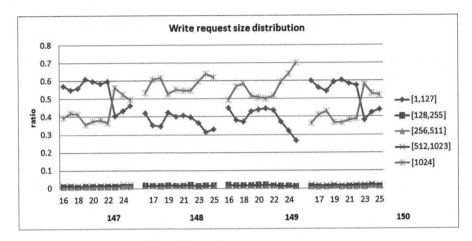

Figure 8-5. *Write request size distribution in different range*

In order to get more insight views into the trace, let's choose a typical piece of a trace (Node 148 and batch 21) with its basic IO properties close to the average value described earlier. Table 8-4 gives the basic information about the workload. Next, I discuss this trace deeply in several aspects, which are summarized in Table 8-3.

Table 8-3. *Summary of Observations and Implications*

SMR characteristics	Hadoop observation
Write once read many	40% read and 60% write Relatively low write update ratio 35.4% stacked ROW ratio
Sequential read to random write	Relatively small random write ratio ROW ratio ~60% and small size, so insignificant impact
Out-of-place update	Stacked WOW: 70% within first 10 minutes Usefulness of large-size SSD/DRAM/AZR cache to performance improvement (write update in cache)
Sequential write	Large size write requests ($S \geq 1024$ blocks) > 64% Mode ratio: write 65% and read 70% Sequential ratio ($S \geq 1024$): write 74% (66%) and read 82% (7%); Near sequential ratio ($S \geq 1024$): write 87% (65%) and read 95% (85%)
Garbage collection (GC)	Frequent small idle time and large idle time periodically Low device utilization Relatively short queue length Relatively low write update ratio 116.3% frequented WOW small write amplification 8.5% write update cmds small rewritten ratio The dominant partial WOW hits are mainly large-size requests, while full hits at small-size requests

Table 8-4. *Basic Statistics of Trace 148-21 (EXT4-WCD)*

	Combined	Read	Write
Number of blocks	917942	373424	544518
Average size (block)	435.7	216.5	586.0
Read IOPS (r/s)			4.322
Write IOPS (w/s)			6.302
Blocks read per second			935.802
Blocks written per second			3693.157

Size and LBA Distribution

The overall request LBA distribution is shown in Figure 8-6a. Figure 8-6b further illustrates the size distribution curve, from which you can see that minimum requests are 8 blocks while the maximum size is 1024 blocks. For write requests, the total ratio of 8-block and 1024-block requests is almost 90%. The ratio of large size write requests ($\geq$1024 blocks) is greater than 55%, so write requests are more sequential. For reads, the ratio of requests with size $\leq$256 is around 50%, and the size distribution is more various. Thus, the read request is generally more random than the write requests. The LBA vs. size distribution figures further confirm this observation. In fact, for writes, you can see that most large size requests lie intensively in few ranges; middle size requests are very few, while for reads, the size distribution is more diverse.

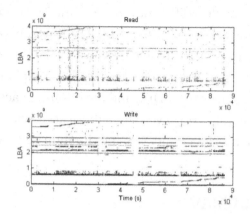

(a) LBA Distribution

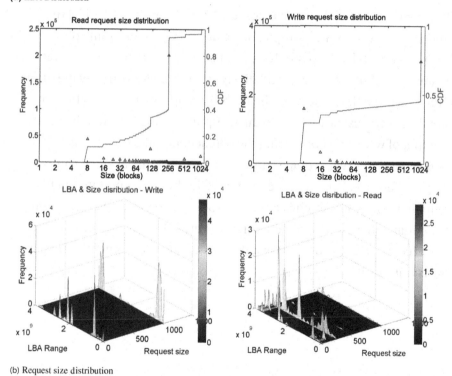

(b) Request size distribution

Figure 8-6. *LBA and size distribution*

These findings provide a different view from the "common sense" of sequential access for Hadoop system [70]. It is true that sequential reads and writes are generated at the HDFS level for large-size files (the settings for chunk size is 128MB), so large-size files are split into 128MB blocks and then stored into the HDFS, and the minimum access unit is therefore 128MB generally. However, when these accesses interact with local file systems such as EXT4 and XFS, the situation becomes much more complex.

IOPS and Throughput

The average value of these two metrics depends on the statistical time window/interval. As an example, burstiness is very commonly observed in this trace, which leads to relatively rigid curves and high maximum IOPS for small time intervals, and a relatively smooth curve with low maximum IOPS for a large time interval. The IOPS for reads are generally higher than that of writes; however, the throughput of reads is generally lower than that of writes. In comparing the 600-second interval average with the 6-second interval average shown in Figure 8-7, the average value has a large difference. Note that the read IOPS in the 6-second interval figure are higher than 400, which is not an "error." The reason is due to the near sequential behavior described earlier. To verify the tool, I compared the parsed curve with the one collected by iostat and iotop, and obtained a consistent result.

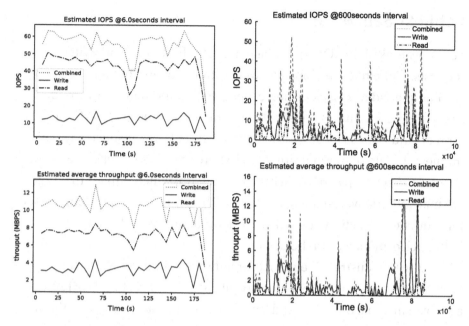

Figure 8-7. *IOPS and throughput*

Utilization and Queue Depth

Both device workload (average 15%) and CPU workload (average 20%)
are low. The average queue depth of the HDD (average value <0.3) further
shows the low device utilization of this workload. As the overall workload
is generally low, and the "periodic" bottom-peak curve is illustrative, the
system therefore can exploit idle time to get the most potential benefits
(such as garbage collection and defragmentation for space efficiency, or
even block reorganization) for performance improvements. However, most
idle time is not long enough for large background jobs. How to fully utilize
these idle times is an interesting topic for future exploration.

Request Sequence

Let's now look at the IO sequential pattern for both read and write requests. Some relevant concepts were introduced in Chapter 2.

For queued next seek distance, observe that the value of the mode (most frequent value) is equal to 0, and the mode ratio at N=64 (N=1) for read and write is 70.2% (61.6%) and 65.4% (61.3%), respectively. This implies a highly sequential workload (where higher is better). The mean absolute value drops quickly with queue length, which implies that there are many interleaved sequence streams. Therefore, the queue length used for sequence detection in a disk drive should be reasonably large to see better performance from the device.

Figure 8-8 illustrates sequence streams with different N, starting from 2 (and doubling to 256). The specific values for N=1 and N=128 are given in Table 8-5 ("w/" and "w/o" denote the cases with or without size constraints). You can see that the streams with only two requests dominate, while the streams with larger request numbers are relatively few. When a size constraint is enforced ($S = 1024$ blocks), the dominate N for read is moved to the value ≥ 3.

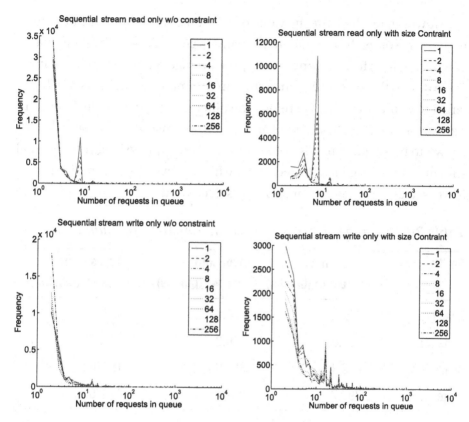

Figure 8-8. *Sequence stream with different N*

Table 8-5. *Sequence Stream and Command Detection*

M2 ≥ 2	Total streams		Total commands	
N=1	w/o	w/	w/o	w/
Read	52827	19987	282911	210081
Write	25633	12412	359668	324007
N=128	w/o	w/	w/o	w/
Read	43682	3579	308149	217373
Write	27303	9209	393962	354384

However, for the write the value of N is still 2. This shift indicates the request size of reads in sequential streams is generally smaller than that of writes. This is further confirmed by the average request size shown in Table 8-6, so the size of sequence stream/commands of writes is much larger than that of reads. Therefore, the difference for read/write between size-constraint ($S = 1024$ blocks) and non-size-constraint requests is shown to be significant. It is noted with increased queue length N, the total stream number is generally decreased while the average stream size is increased and average command size is decreased.

Table 8-6. *Average Size of Sequence Stream and Command*

Op (N)	Avg. cmd size w/o (blocks)	Avg. cmd size w/ (blocks)	Avg. stream size w/ (blocks)
Read (1)	259.5	308.9	3247.3
Write (1)	952.0	910.3	24851.7
Read (128)	245.4	307.9	18700.5
Write (128)	797.7	882.2	31685.2

The total sequence stream detected is illustrated in Figure 8-9. This figure shows that the write request is much more sequential than read (considering the ratio). Note that for this figure, "combined" is not a simple sum of "read" and "write;" it is detected in the FIFO rule with all commands. The value displayed in Table 8-5 is consistent to the mode counter of queued next seek distance. In fact, you can easily calculate that the frequency of mode is the total command number of streams minus the total number of streams.

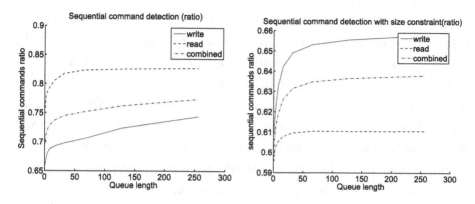

Figure 8-9. *Sequence ratio with S=1024*

Therefore, you can see that total ratio of "sequential" read/write is over 82% and 74% (N=256), respectively (detected read/write sequential commands/total write/read commands), without size constraints. The ratio is reduced to 76% and 65.5%, respectively, with the size constraint (S =1024), which is more reasonable to indicate the sequence ratio.

With increased S, the ratio of sequential read/write commands drops slightly, as shown in Figure 8-10. It shows that the sequence of write is rather strong, as the sequence streams are generally large, so the ratio of writes is reduced from 82% to 62% and 58% when S is changed from 1024 to 4096 and 8196, respectively.

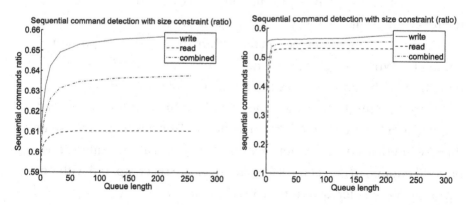

Figure 8-10. *Sequence ratio with with S=4096 and 8192*

As shown in Figure 8-11, near-sequential for read is very strong. The total ratio for writes and reads is over 87% and 95%, respectively (detected write or read sequential commands/total write or read commands), without considering size constraint. It reduces to 65% and 85%, respectively, with the size constraint, which is more reasonable to indicate the sequence ratio of reads is higher than that of writes. With increased S, the ratio of near-sequential read/write commands slightly drops, similar to that of sequence ratio. Note that the distance is generally larger than 8 blocks; when $\delta d \geq 16$, the increment is significant.

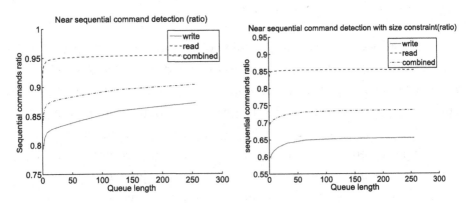

Figure 8-11. *Near sequence ratio with S=1024*

All the (near) sequence information discussed above provides a good reference for pre-fetch policy design for disk drives. For example, when considering a sequence detection algorithm, the gap is an important parameter. When designing a hot data identification algorithm, the definition of hit frequency may be changed slightly for these near sequence streams. For instance, the LBA hit within a certain region can be counted as a hot area to take post-read action. The observations also tell that the interleaved stream number is not large and a small queue may be good enough to detect the sequence (e.g., N≥16, compared with non-cache, N=50 can increase around 5% sequence).

Write Update

For frequent write updates, 86% of accessed blocks (maybe repeated) are only written once. A decreasing percentage of written blocks are written multiple times, which means only a small portion of hot blocks are rewritten. Write amplification is roughly 116.3% if all rewritten data is put into a new place.

For a timed write update, total write blocks occur 80% of total access blocks (read and write), and the updated blocks (at least write twice) are only 6.8%. Total write commands are 59% of the total commands and the update commands are 22.5%. The average size of write commands is around 586 blocks and the average size of overlapped blocks of update commands is 73.3.

Before you look at the stacked write update, check the stacked distance first. You will find that small requests have a high probability to be full hits as opposed to large sized request (since the hit size is much smaller than the average size). In fact, the average overlapped sizes for partial hits (only a part of blocks are the same) and full hits (two requests are the same) are 139.4 and 55.1 blocks, respectively. You can conclude that a partial hit is more likely to happen for large size requests by using the numbers in Tables 8-4 and 8-7.

Table 8-7. *Statistics for Logical Stack Distance (LSD)*

	LSD≤1000	LSD≤2000	LSD≤4000	Overall
Partial, Full	2.8%, 14.9%	3.5%, 17.6%	4.4%, 19.9%	7.5%, 27.3%

A further check can be obtained by considering the full and partial hits separately by referring to Figure 8-12 for the hit frequency vs. LBA and size. This confirms the dominant partial hit at large size, while full hit at small size. The hits of the requests with medium-size (64-1023 blocks) are much less.

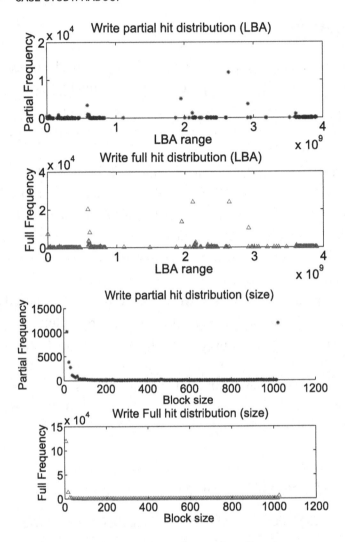

Figure 8-12. *Write update LBA and size distribution*

Now let's check stacked write update ratio. Based on write IOPS, distance 4000 is roughly 10 minutes. In this period, you can see 72.9% full write hit and 58.7% partial write hit of commands. With the knowledge of cache size and structure, you can estimate the hit ratio. As the stack distance is generally longer than DRAM cache length, updates on disk cannot be avoided. Therefore, a "caching/buffering" location on the media is necessary, so a larger-size SSD cache is necessary for performance improvement.

The third plot in Figure 8-13 shows that over 65% of the overlapped request size happens in the first 1% of overall time for partial/full hits, which further confirms the necessity of large SSD cache. As conventional disk drives have not provided such a big cache, it may be beneficial to implement this cache via a hybrid drive (SSD+HDD) or at a higher level in the system, such as array controllers or aggregate controllers. For SMR drive, a convenient way is to allow conventional zones accompanying with shingled zones for random write access.[3] It is also called random access zone (RAZ) in [5, 4].

---

[3]For more information, please refer to T10.org and T13.org, such as zoned block commands (ZBC)

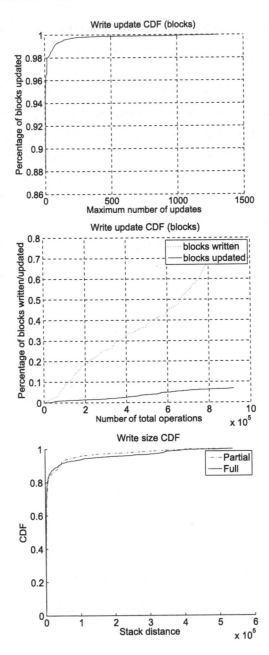

Figure 8-13. *Frequented, timed, and stacked write update (from top to bottom)*

Read on Write (ROW)

ROW ratio is mainly used to check if "write once read many (WORM)" is possible. You will find that the total ROW ratio is around 35.4% only, which implied that the written data is less likely to be read multiple times (i.e., a ratio much larger than 1). You can further check if the hit is only for small size requests. Figures 8-14 and 8-15 show that the written data is less likely to be immediately read back for most cases for similar reasons as explained in previous chapters.

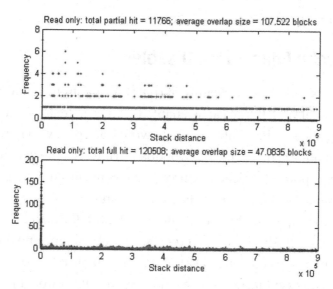

Figure 8-14. *ROW ratio*

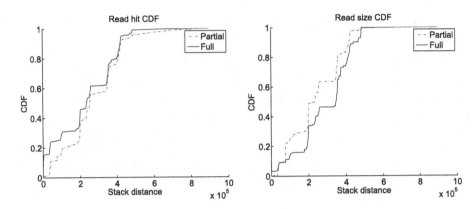

Figure 8-15. *ROW hit and size distribution*

Write Cache Enabled vs. Disabled

Write cache is an important feature of HDDs. Many studies show that the performance of WCE (write cache enabled) can be increased significantly over WCD (write cache disabled) due to write-back policy, in particular for some small-size random write workloads. However, the data reliability concern (e.g., power loss leads to dirty data loss in DRAM write cache) results in most data centers disabling this feature.

Here we compare four traces (148-21, 148-22, 149-21, and 149-22) as nodes 148 and 149 always use different write cache setting and there is a setting change between batch ID 21 and 22 (see Table 8-2). You can see that there is no essential difference among write IOPS, throughput, and average size as shown in Table 8-8. Meanwhile, the ratio of large write requests (e.g., 1024 blocks) almost remains the same. Nevertheless, you can observe that the (near) sequence ratio of WCD is slightly smaller than that of WCE for both reads and writes (1% of absolute value). These factors show that the HDFS does not change its behavior according to HDD's write cache settings, even though the local file system may respond to it. However, as the workload is far away from the drive's boundary capability, the response is not significant.

Table 8-8. *Basic IO metrics for WCD vs. WCE*

Average	IOPS		Throughput KBPS		Size blocks	
	21	22	21	22	21	22
148	6.3	7.0	1846.6	2064.4	586.0	589.5
149	6.6	6.8	1782.2	1881.9	541.8	556.6

In the heavy workload cases, some interleaved sequential streams will be considered as "random" rather than sequential, causing an increased ratio of random writes, which is harmful to the overall disk performance. Therefore, some non-volatile memory or DRAM protection technologies may be applied in order to enable write cache, which becomes necessary for heavy workloads. Additionally, for green environments in data centers where the bottleneck is not the HDDs (at least under normal workloads), another benefit to WCE is energy savings due to less mechanical accesses to the HDDs.

System-Level View

In this section, I present a brief analysis of how the random IO, observed in the previous section, of the block level traces led to a better analysis of the Hadoop cluster's IO patterns. First, let's look at the workload characteristics collected from HDFS logs, as shown in Table 8-9. Recall the system level analysis mentioned earlier; I captured data generation and deletion rates, job creation rates and characteristics, etc. with the low level IO obfuscated from us. Arguably, this is how a high-level framework should behave, fully or mostly insulated from the hardware devices below. However, those who have to maintain the full operational stack must be aware of the entire system, not just the user-level framework. Below, I analyze the randomness from three aspects: the Hadoop framework, the MapReduce policy, and HDFS mechanism.[4]

---

[4]Grant Markey made some contributions to this and the conclusion section.

Table 8-9. *Basic Information Collected from HDFS Logs*

Name	Duration	Total IO Requests			Average IO Size(MB)		
		Ave	Max	Min	Total	Read	Write
wdc-x1	68 d	0.627	5.476	0.125	60.96	3.14	99.75
wdc-x2	98 d	0.396	5.661	0.107	47.83	3.09	93.2
	R/W ratio			IOPS 10^5			Throughput (MB/S)		
Avg	Max	Min	Total	Read	Write	Total	Read	Write
0.0348	0.125	0.0054	0.726	0.536	0.19	18.48	0.632	17.85
0.0383	0.33	0.007	0.458	0.325	0.133	12.11	0.442	11.67

Notice that all daemons within the Hadoop framework write logs of their runtime throughout the course of the day. Depending on configuration, this can be written to the HDFS or to the local FS. If logs are written to the local FS, they account for some random IO to the HDD. Other daemons of frameworks which sit on top of Hadoops core framework can generate more random IOs at the device level. Hbase has similar logs from its region servers which must be written. Created for real-time data processing, Hbase will spawn small MapReduce jobs which access potentially small amounts of data, causing random read IOs in a HDFS instance. Frameworks like Hive and other KV stores, which sit on top of Hadoop, have similar logging structures which can potentially cause random IO amplification down at the device level.

Java-based (apache) MapReduce must write temporary intermediary files to disk during MapReduce jobs, some with repeating process IDs (PIDs) and others with single or minimal use PIDs. These intermediary files can either be dumped to locations in the HDFS (which attempts to serialize the IO if possible) or the local FS, which will be a random IO event. This is configurable via tuning the parameter `mapreduce.task.tmp.dir`.

After consulting the Hadoop XML configuration files, one thing that I noticed was that the temporary/intermediary space for all HDFS and

MapReduce workloads were configured to store their output data to the HDFS data drive. Because the Hadoop framework is written in Java, it must contend with the properties of the Java Virtual Machine (JVM), meaning that memory addresses have no meaning between JVMs. Hence, when a MapReduce task passes data to another MapReduce task, it first writes data to a temporary file for the other JVM task to read. Additionally, when a MapReduce job launches, it must send the configuration parameters and executable jar file to the TaskTrackers so that they can correctly spawn map and reduce tasks. This data too was being stored to that configured local temporary space.

Couple this IO with the observation that the cluster runs close to 5500 MapReduce jobs per day, of which many are small task count jobs (due to the 20% HBase analysis performed by users), and the amount of random IO generated on these HDDs becomes very large. However, this IO is something that can be mitigated and was not completely responsible for the high level of random IO seen in the block-level traces. The HDFS itself also contributes to the amount of random IO seen in those traces.

From the system logs as shown in Figure 8-16, you can see that the number of chunks created and deleted daily is quite high for the system. Each time the HDFS commits a chunk of data to the filesystem, it also creates a metadata file. This metadata file is proportional to the size of the HDFS chunk committed to the localFS, so a 128MB chunk will have a corresponding ≈1.2MB metadata file created where smaller chunks will have smaller metadata files. Hence, for the observed workload, there is a lot of small random IO due to tens of thousands of new chunks being generated daily on the HDFS. However, unlike the observed random IO for the MapReduce framework, wherein the location to store the temporary files is configurable, the location where these HDFS metadata files are stored is not a configurable property, and therefore cannot be delegated to another class of storage or storage location. When considering newer HDD technologies, wherein random IO (especially random writes) can greatly impact performance, understanding workload characteristics like these are paramount. Without a device-level analysis of the workload, these characteristics would have not been so clearly identified.

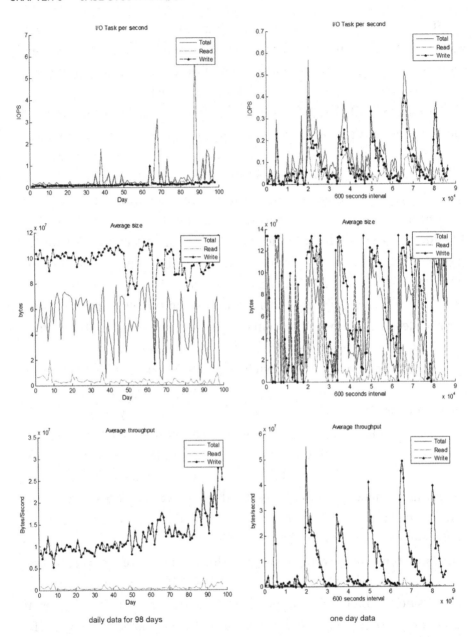

Figure 8-16. *Basic curves from HDFS logs*

Some Further Discussions

In this chapter, I presented the block-level workload characteristics of the Hadoop cluster by considering some specific metrics. The analysis techniques presented can help others understand the performance and drive characteristics of Hadoop in their production environments. Collected by blktrace, I conducted a comprehensive analysis of these logs which identified new workload patterns with some unexpected behaviors. I showed that, while sequential and near-sequential requests represent the majority of the IO workload, a non-trivial amount of random IO requests exist in the Hadoop workloads. Additionally, the write update ratio on drives is not very high, which indicates that a small write amplification can occur if an out-of-place write policy is applied. Also note that the ROW ratio is small, which means WORM does not generally hold for the cluster's workload. All these findings imply a relatively high spatial locality and lower-than-expected temporal locality, which show that Hadoop is generally a suitable application for SMR drives. However, further improvements in both Hadoop and drive sides are required.

Looking critically at the configuration of a Hadoop system, it is possible to fine-tune and minimize some, but not all, of the observed random IO. Factors that add to this random IO are several types of framework logging, intermediary files generated by MapReduce and HBase workloads, and metadata files of HDFS chunks. The verbosity of Hadoop daemon log files can be turned down to generate less data, and they along with temporary MapReduce output can be written to a storage location which will not impact HDFS chunk IO operations. Among these can be the HDFS itself (rather than local storage), which will attempt to make the IO more sequential, or on another physical/logical block device more suited to random block IO (while maintaining data locality). Some basic curves derived from HDFS logs are shown in Figure 8-16.

However, the final piece of the observed random IO is a consequence of HDFS write/update mechanism and cannot be easily mitigated because it currently must reside with the committed HDFS chunks on the HDFS data drives. The small IO caused by chunk metadata must then be serviced by a capacity block storage device which can either understand how to transform these small random IO into larger sequential access patterns, or a device that is simply designed to handle random IO. Without a device-level view, it is possible that this overhead would be dismissed as a problem elsewhere in the system rather than at the HDD device level, where some of these issues are very simple to correct, given the proper insight. For instance, a large DRAM buffer will be very useful for these scenarios with random read accesses, and non-volatile memory (e.g., NAND and conventional zone) for these random write accesses.

Hence, it is reasonable to study an integration of HDFS and the local files systems with consideration of device properties, such as a design in a global view so that there is no "misunderstanding" of the local metadata to the sequential write in HDFS. And the metadata and the "non-critical" intermediate/temporary data are assigned to proper disk location. Therefore, HDFS could take the responsibility of file/block accesses in DataNode, which may make the drive operation more efficient. The metadata location in the device shall also be carefully designed.

In addition, the drive-level cache and system-level cache may be unified with the consideration of the mechanism of Java, such that some temporary data may be absorbed by the unified cache/buffer instead of disk mechanical accesses. This unification could be difficult due to the current HDFS's simple cache design and lack of direct interface between JVM and drives. However, it is possible for drive manufacturers to provide such an application-oriented interface for communication.

Furthermore, a certain intelligence might be useful for the drive to understand the nature of the access (e.g., random or sequential, access dependency), such that the drive can immediately switch to the optimal algorithm/behavior for better performance. An application-level hinting scheme with interaction between host and drive or a self-learning algorithm inside drive can be helpful.

In conclusion, the device level analysis of the in-house Hadoop cluster has provided new insights into how Hadoop interacts with the underlying file system and handles its lower-level IO. These new insights motivate me to continue studying how workload characteristics of big data frameworks and application tuning could help the performance of storage devices in the current data driven climate which we live in. This study is also applicable to Spark, an in-memory MapReduce system roughly. For example, a detailed workload analysis can provide some insights of the SCM application for Spark systems, which will benefit a cost-efficient design of hybrid SCM-DRAM structures.

CHAPTER 9

Case Study: Ceph

Ceph, an open-source distributed storage platform, provides a unified interface for object-, block-, and file-level storage [33, 80, 34, 81]. This chapter presents the block-level workload characteristics of a WD WASP/ EPIC microserver-based Ceph cluster. The analysis techniques presented can help you to understand the performance and drive characteristics of Ceph in production environments. In addition, I also identify whether SMR, hybrid disk, and SSD drives are suitable for the Ceph workload.

The basic architecture of Ceph was described in Chapter 1. Ceph's core, RADOS, is a fully distributed, reliable, and autonomous object store using the CRUSH (Controlled Replication Under Scalable Hashing) algorithm. Ceph's building blocks are called OSDs (object storage daemons). OSDs are responsible for storing objects on local file systems (e.g., EXT4 and XFS), and cooperating to replicate data, detect and recover from failures, or migrate data when OSDs join or leave the cluster. Ceph's design originated in the premise that failures are common in large-scale storage systems. Along these lines, Ceph targets at guaranteeing reliability and scalability by leveraging the intelligence of the OSDs. Each OSD uses a journal to accelerate the write operations by coalescing small writes and flushing them asynchronously to the backing file system when the journal is full. The journal can be a different file or located in another device or partition [82, 83, 84].

© Jun Xu 2018
J. Xu, *Block Trace Analysis and Storage System Optimization*,
https://doi.org/10.1007/978-1-4842-3928-5_9

These tests are based on a "unique" platform. Instead of traditional workstations, the so-called microserver structure is used for the production environments. In the system, each microserver has an individual OS and an HDD. It is almost the minimum granularity for an IO device, which essentially satisfies the original design requirement of Sage Weil, the father of Ceph [80, 33]. In fact, this architecture minimizes the failure domain to a disk unit instead of many disks becoming inaccessible in one server with a multi-disk architecture. The storage cluster is scaled out by connection microservers by a top of the rack Ethernet switch.

A microserver-based cluster with 12 nodes (named as sm1-wasp1 to sm1-wasp12) is shown in Figure 9-1. Three virtual machines (VMs) act as the clients to generate the IO requests (named as Cag-blaster-ixgbe-02 to Cag-blasterixgbe-04). All the tests are done in the Ceph version Jewel. In this microserver-based configuration for filestore, each node/drive is divided into four partitions. /dev/sda1 installs the operating system (Ubuntu) and /dev/sda3 is reserved. /dev/sda2 is used for metadata, and /dev/sda4 is used for user data.

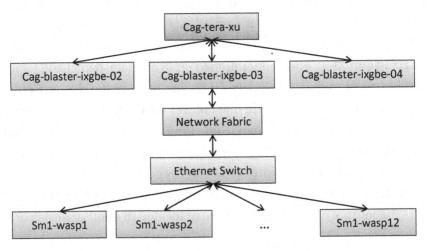

Figure 9-1. *Ceph cluster topology*

Filestore IO Pattern

Three VMs are used as clients to send bench write requests to a replicate pool (named rep1 with one replicate) for 250 seconds and blktrace to collect traces for 310 seconds, so `rados bench -p rep1 250 write` from each client and `blktrace /dev/sdax -w 310` from each node. Due to the limitation of blktrace (it's unable to collect an individual partition in the same drive), the trace from sda2/sda4 and the whole sda are collected separately. A bus analyzer is also used to verify the traces.

The common properties of the 12 nodes are listed in Table 9-1. You can observe that the basic properties are generally similar. One of the IO pattern curves is illustrated in Figures 9-2 and 9-3, where the three rows represent sda2, sda4, and sda, respectively. Note that all wasp nodes are write cache enabled. The command of `"ceph tell osd.* bench 41943040 4194304"` gives around 100MBPS (cached). Therefore, it means the three clients with 32 threads each have almost fully utilized the disk bandwidth. The reason will be explained later.

You can also see that differences of IO patterns may still exist in different nodes; for example, the read/write ratio is high in some nodes while it is low in other nodes, and the idle time distribution varies. Based on read/write ratio, we can roughly divide the IO patterns into two classes: one is read dominated, and the other is write dominated. When read dominates, the average size of the read becomes smaller.

Table 9-1. *Common Properties for Ceph Nodes*

Properties	Metadata	Data
R/W	Mixed read and write	No read requests
Size	Relatively small requests (8-block requests dominated); size of write varies largely; the R/W ratio varies largely.	1024-block requests dominated, followed by small blocks
Sequence	Mode =8 (very small); relatively more random over a small range. Much higher near sequential ratio than strict sequential ratio (small gaps exist for 50% requests)	Mode =0; high sequential ratio. Higher near sequential ratio (small gaps exist for 5% write requests)
Write update	High update ratio (>50% write requests updated)	Low update ratio (updated blocks <1%, more partial)
Write stack distance	Relatively small distance to achieve high percentage of hits; small average overlap size (8 blocks); necessary for write cache.	Relatively large distance to achieve high percentage of hits; small average overlap size; unnecessary for write cache.

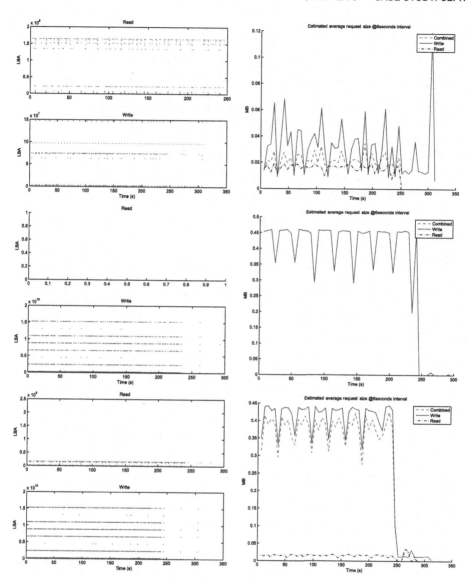

Figure 9-2. *IO pattern in different partitions: LBA and size distribution*

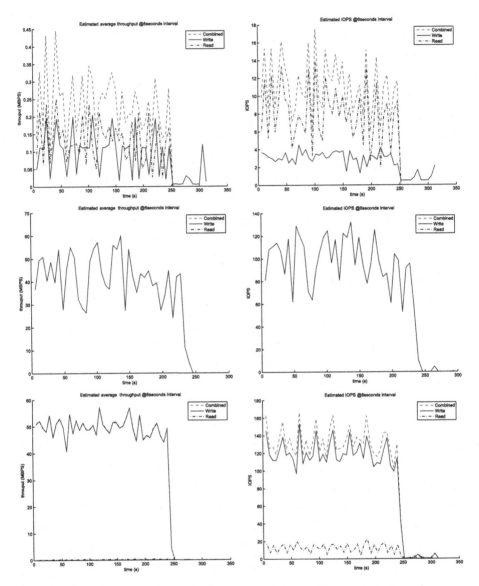

Figure 9-3. *IO pattern in different partitions: Throughput and IOPS*

Table 9-2 shows the total idle time for different nodes at different scenarios. Basically, the idle time is unevenly distributed, which means that the workload to each node is actually uneven. In other words, some nodes are very busy, such as wasp12 in the case of "3-8" (3 clients, 8 threads), while some are very "lazy," such as wasp8 in the case of "3-8." This is partially due to the CRUSH algorithm, which is in charge of PG (placement group) allocations. Although a reasonable number of clients and threads may alleviate the uneven distribution, it may not essentially solve this problem. Thus, some improvement policies, such as asynchronized, active feedback, adjustable PG, etc, shall be implemented.

Table 9-2. *Total Idle Time in the First 240 Seconds*

CT	wasp4	wasp5	wasp6	wasp7	wasp8	wasp9	wasp10	wasp11	wasp12	mean	std	std/mean	max/min
3-8	52.48	17.77	55.34	44.65	114.21	9.1	48.49	21.13	0.7	40.43	34.17	0.85	162.2
3-16	107.78	0.15	76.31	113.58	0.85	39.87	5.91	22.52	61.66	47.63	44.53	0.93	746.81
3-32	48.09	63.42	35.93	4.19	8.45	0.01	25.61	0	4.87	21.17	23.34	1.1	895803
3-64	69.69	37.38	79.85	33.21	32.67	30.81	29.85	31.31	30.2	41.66	19.07	0.46	2.68
1-8	150.49	15.65	130.66	0.31	7.65	5.34	127.56	1.01	5.18	49.32	65.63	1.33	488.16
1-16	21.65	5.19	48.3	151.41	39.05	2.13	19.54	37.68	17.54	38.05	45.22	1.19	71.03
1-32	8.13	5.59	95.29	32.94	6.36	9.03	78.46	102.52	42.2	42.28	39.91	0.94	18.34
1-64	17.03	114.01	58.21	1.23	32.77	17.55	9.72	6.1	36.54	32.57	35.32	1.08	92.77

Performance Consistency Verification

Performance consistency is a basic requirement for enterprise storage systems and it guarantees the performance repeatability at the same conditions. There are several approaches to check it. Table 9-3 gives a summary.

Table 9-3. *Comparison of Three Approaches*

Metrics	Pro	Con
Hypothesis	Full view with relatively full information; consistency in a relatively strict sense.	Hardly satisfied
Average only	Simple and relatively easily satisfied	Partial view with limited information on average only
Range tolerance	Engineer's view in practice; easy to check.	Partial view; usually experiment dependent.

The first one is the hypothesis approach, which actually can be used to test whether two or more samples have the same mean (and variance), median, or distribution in statistical sense. A simple procedure is as follows:

1. Check if all rounds of tests have steady state.

2. Use the steady state of each round as a sample vector for an overall consistency test or one-two-one (paired) test.

3. Select a proper hypothesis test for different requirements/assumptions.

Some common hypothesis tests are used in different scenarios:

- **F-test:** Requires each sample vector is normal distribution; if the final p-value is smaller than predefined significant level (0.05 by default), you reject the hypothesis that these samples have the same mean.

- **H-test:** Requires each sample vector is continuous distribution (weaker condition); if the final p-value is smaller than predefined significant level (0.05 by default), you reject the hypothesis that these samples have the same median.

- **T-test:** Applicable for paired independent tests only; if the final p-value is smaller than predefined significant level (0.05 by default), you reject the hypothesis that these samples have the same distribution.

This approach actually gives the result in a relatively strict sense. However, you may allow some differences in most cases.

The second one uses a simplified statistical method, which only concerns the average value without the overall trend, and is usually for rough estimation only:

1. Get the average values of interested metrics of each test (possibly in steady state).

2. Form a sample vector with the average values from all rounds.

3. Test if it follows a normal distribution (or other experimental distribution, such as uniform) with an acceptable variance.

The third one is the range tolerance approach, which checks if the performance is within a certain region that we can tolerant/allow experimentally:

1. Check if each run's value is within a certain range of this run's mean or expected experimental value. There are two cases: one is required for all data points, such as latency, and the other is only required for almost all points, such as throughput.

2. Check if the average value of each run is within a certain range of the mean of all runs.

This approach usually needs the experts to set up the proper thresholds in order to construct a reasonable range.

Let's take a look at an example with seven rounds of tests in the same environments in Table 9-4. Each round contains three random read and three sequential write accesses. Since an F-test requires normality, you begin with the normal test on each round. In some cases, if you cannot not capture enough data, you may simply mark it as invalid. In this example, you can see only two rounds out of seven pass the normal test for the test named rand 6, and the two rounds likely have the same mean. Overall, the results indicate that the performance is not strictly consistent.

Table 9-4. An Example of the Hypothesis Approach

Value	rand_6	rand_4	rand_2	write_5	write_3	write_1
Normal	2	3	2	6	0	2
Non-normal	5	3	5	1	7	5
Invalid	0	1	0	0	0	0
F-value	3.114	60.405	3.261	24.002	24.002	57.901
P-value	0.079	0	0.073	0	−1	0
Result	1	0	1	0	−1	0

If you switch to average-only and range tolerance approaches, you may have another observation in a relaxed sense, shown in Tables 9-5 and 9-6. Table 9-5 shows the average throughput in MBPS for each round, as well as the overall mean and standard derivation. Table 9-6 shows the difference ratio between each round and the overall average. You can see most ratios are within 10%. If the customers can allow a 20% range, you may say that the system satisfies the performance consistency requirement. Note that curve of each round shall also satisfy some range requirements in a "continuous" sense. Figure 9-4 shows one example of six tests. Table 9-7 gives the ratio that the total number of values fall into the range of ± 20% or ± 10% of the mean. If a 20% range is set, you can see that only the test named write 5 doesn't satisfy the requirements.

Table 9-5. Summary for Bandwidth of Rados Bench

Mean	rand_6	rand_4	rand_2	write_5	write_3	write_1
R0	679.72	1642.15	1613.56	327.86	1261.88	405.87
R1	704.20	1596.64	1446.77	345.57	1275.05	386.54
R2	814.66	1646.67	1503.92	397.04	1322.19	442.87
R3	907.08	1566.22	1529.88	401.05	1225.51	394.28
R4	891.53	1539.09	1399.01	409.12	1200.37	360.88
R5	902.05	1507.67	1194.60	416.98	1310.67	422.73
R6	762.12	1524.56	1164.23	361.48	1186.59	336.50
Mean	808.77	1574.71	1407.42	379.87	1254.61	392.81
Std	88.65	51.49	157.14	32.06	48.69	33.39
Std/Mean	0.11	0.03	0.11	0.08	0.04	0.09

Table 9-6. *Comparison via Range Tolerance Approach*

Diff Ratio	rand_6	rand_4	rand_2	write_5	write_3	write_1
R0	−0.160	0.043	0.146	−0.137	0.006	0.033
R1	−0.129	0.014	0.028	−0.090	0.016	−0.016
R2	0.007	0.046	0.069	0.045	0.054	0.127
R3	0.122	−0.005	0.087	0.056	−0.023	0.004
R4	0.102	−0.023	−0.006	0.077	−0.043	−0.081
R5	0.115	−0.043	−0.151	0.098	0.045	0.076
R6	−0.058	−0.032	−0.173	−0.048	−0.054	−0.143
Max	0.122	0.046	0.146	0.098	0.054	0.127
Min	−0.129	−0.043	−0.173	−0.137	−0.054	−0.143

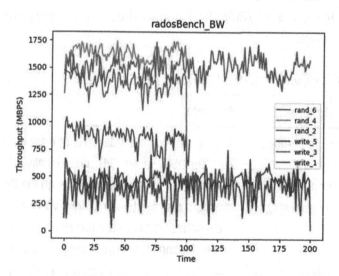

Figure 9-4. *Bandwidth from six tests in one round*

Table 9-7. *Ratio of Values within a Given Range Around Mean*

Ratio	rand_6	rand_4	rand_2	write_5	write_3	write_1
± 0.2	0.91	1	0.99	0.44	1	0.9
± 0.1	0.73	0.99	0.89	0.2	0.91	0.6

Bottleneck Identification

Ceph is a rather complex system whose performance is decided by both hardware and software [41]. From the hardware point of view, CPU, memory, disk, and network are the four major components. Tables 9-8 and 9-9 give some general views. From the software aspect, there are even more factors, such as the file system, Linux OS settings, memory allocator, and more. In addition, the Ceph system configuration provides hundreds of parameters, and many of them affect the overall performance. Therefore, it is generally difficult to identify the performance bottleneck of the overall system.

Table 9-8. *Impact of CPU, Memory, and Network*

Variables	Options	Remarks
CPU	Core number, speed, structure, instruct set, etc.	A common recommendation is at least one (virtual) core per OSD. Faster CPU cores usually help in performance improvement, although the CPU structure also matters (e.g., Intel vs. ARM, internal architecture/versions) the real perf/GB, perf/$, and so on. Turning off energy-saving mode helps.
Memory	RAM per server, RAM per OSD, etc.	A common recommendation is at least 1GB per 1TB OSD, and better 2GB per OSD. The actual value is workload-dependent.

(continued)

Table 9-8. (*continued*)

Variables	Options	Remarks
BIOS	HT mode, energy-saving, NUMA, etc.	HT affects the virtual core number (enable). Consider the tradeoff of energy-savings for low power but less computational resource allocated.
Network switch/NIC	Bandwidth and latency; Ethernet, Fiber, Infiniband, etc.	Higher bandwidth for higher throughput to an extent; lower latency for more small IO. Try ms crc data = false and ms crc header = false for high-quality networks. For cluster with less than 20 spinners or 2 SSDs, consider upgrading to a 25GbE or 40GbE.

Table 9-9. *Impact of Disk*

Variables	Options	Remarks
Drive type	HDD, SSD, NVM, etc.	Balance between price and performance shall be considered; usually SSD acts as cache and journal; unbalanced structure may lead to performance loss; one bad drive can affect the overall pool performance (ceph osd perf).
Drive number	Drive per server, drive per OSD	More drives increase throughput per server but decrease throughput per OSD; one OSD per platter/drive.
Drive controller	SAS/ SATA/ PCIe HBA, etc.	More/better HBAs increase throughput. HW RAID may increase IOPS. The best performance is achieved when you have one HBA for every 6-8 SAS drives, but it is cheaper to use a SAS expander to let one HBA control 24 (or more) drives. More HBAs and fewer expanders are used to achieve maximum throughput, or SAS expanders can be applied to minimize cost when full drive throughput is not needed.

(*continued*)

Table 9-9. (*continued*)

Variables	Options	Remarks
RAID controller	Enable/ disable; cache	More recent testing with Red Hat, Supermicro, and Seagate also showed that a good RAID controller with onboard write-back cache can accelerate IOPS-oriented write performance. While Ceph does not use RAID (since it supports both simple replication and EC), the right RAID controller cache can still improve write performance via the onboard cache.
Drive cache	Enable or disable write cache	Cache has large impact on small write performance

In this sense, you shall monitor all necessary components of the system in order to make a conclusion. Take the Ceph software stack as an example in Figure 9-5. You may deploy the corresponding system monitoring tools [1] into interested stack points to collect data so that you can capture all possible places for SW failures, errors, performance degrades, etc. plus all potential SW performance tuning points. In fact, Ceph has some built-in monitoring tools such as LTTng.

---

[1]See Brendan Gregg's chart of general Linux performance tools at www.brendangregg.com/linuxperf.html.

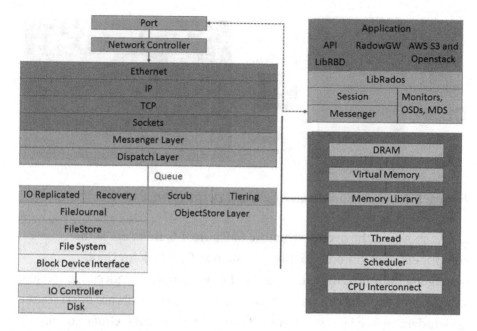

Figure 9-5.   *Ceph software stack*

Dedicated tools for Ceph deployment, monitoring, and management have been developed, such as CeTune (Intel),[2] VSM (Intel),[3] OpenATTIC,[4] and InkScope.[5]

With the aid of some integrated tools, such as SaltStack,[6] you may design your own all-in-one tool. Figure 9-6 shows one possible design, which intends to integrate the functionalities of configuration, deployment, benchmarking, and measurement analysis of Ceph systems. It can be developed by using the "glue" programming language Python, together with some Bash scripts.

---

[2]https://github.com/01org/CeTune
[3]https://github.com/01org/virtual-storage-manager
[4]www.OpenATTIC.org
[5]https://github.com/inkscope/inkscope
[6]https://saltstack.com/

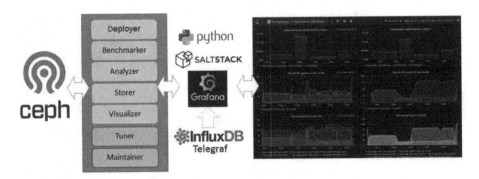

Figure 9-6. *Functionalities of a Ceph performance tool*

As shown in the overall structure of Figure 9-6, there are some components integrated into this tool, such as SaltStack for Ceph management, InfluxDB[7] with Telegraf[8] for performance data collection and storage, and Grafana[9] for data visualization. All these tools are open source and under the free license (InfluxDB/Telegraf under MIT, Grafana/salt-stack under Apache v2).

SaltStack platform or Salt is an open-source configuration management software and remote execution engine in Python. It essentially has a server-client structure. You can use Salt to manage the Ceph nodes and distribute executing commands. InfluxDB is a time series database built from scratch to handle high write and query loads. Telegraf, developed by Go,[10] is a metric collection daemon that can gather metrics from a wide array of inputs and write them into a wide group of outputs. It is plugin-driven for both the collection and output of data for easy extension. It is a compiled and standalone binary that can be executed on any system without external dependencies; no npm/pip/gem or other package management tools required. Once Telegraf daemon is running,

---

[7]www.influxdata.com/

[8]www.influxdata.com/time-series-platform/telegraf/

[9]https://grafana.com/

[10]https://golang.org/

the data will be automatically saved to influxDB. Grafana provides a powerful and exquisite way to create, explore, and share dashboards and information with your team and the world. After the DBs are set up, you can configure Grafanas data sources from these influxDB.

With this tool, you can easily obtain all necessary information. Take a look at the example provided in the section on the filesstore IO pattern. From Table 9-2, you can clearly observe that some drives are drained of IO bandwidth. However, the CPU, memory and network usages are all lower than 50% at the same time. Therefore, you can make a conclusion that the drives are the performance bottleneck.

APPENDIX A

Tools and Functions

In this appendix, trace analysis tools based on MATLAB [85] and Python [86] are introduced. The functionalities are explained and sample code is provided. Although these two tools use different languages, they generally have common interfaces, such as the same input and output parameters.

MATLAB-Based Tool: MBPAR

The MATLAB-based Block-Trace Parser, Analyzer and Reporter (MBPAR) is designed for easy use.[1] Without specified options, the default setting will do all the available analysis and output all the analyzed results into a Microsoft PowerPoint (ppt) file. The intermediate figures and data can be also saved into disk for next usage. Sample code is as follows:

```
%  define the filename to parse and analyze
filename= D :\sample. t r c
%  parse the blktrace file and translate the events into MATLAB
matrix
blktrace_parser;
%  analyze the IO events with/without raw report
```

---

[1]https://github.com/junxuwdc/MBPAR. Jun Xu developed most of the code, while Junpeng Niu contributed few functions on sequential analysis.

© Jun Xu 2018
J. Xu, *Block Trace Analysis and Storage System Optimization*,
https://doi.org/10.1007/978-1-4842-3928-5

```
batch_analysis;
% generate report in a given PowerPoint format
batch_generate_ppt;
```

Here the files `blktrace parser.m`, `batch analysis.m`, and `batch generate ppt.m` are all scripts. We use scripts for simplicity, although they can be easily converted into functions. For example, `blktrace parser.m` receives the filename of raw traces as input and output the parsed IO events as the input of `batch analysis.m`, which further output analyzed results and figures as input of `batch generate ppt.m`.

The output of `blktrace parser.m` mainly contains two variables: 1) `lists_cmd` is a N × 3 matrix, where N is the number of requests, and 3 columns represents the first LBA, the size, and the type (0 for write and 1 for read) of the request, respectively; 2) `lists_action` is a N × 2 matrix, which represents the arrival time and completion time of requests. Note that the input for the analysis functions can be from any type of traces other than blktrace, as long as the data format is the same for `lists_cmd` and `lists_action`.

The content of `batch_analysis.m` is straightforward. Essentially, it defines some data formats and calls all available analysis functions. There are some parameters (including these for subfunctions of analysis) to adjust the tool's behavior:

- `options.offset time` is used to adjust the starting time of the traces. In some traces, the starting time does not start from 0 so you need to find the starting time of the first event. The default value is 0.

- `options.time interval` indicates the time window when calculating the average value in seconds. The default value is 1 second.

- `options.plot figure` decides if the tool outputs a figure. When `options.export report` is true, `options.plot figure` will be set as true too.

- options.plot fontsize regulates the font size used in the figure.

- options.export report decides if a debug report with raw data and figures is generated. This option is only used in Windows system for debug purpose.

- options.report name indicates the debug report name.

- options.near_sequence configures whether a strict sequential stream (0) or a near sequential stream (1) is calculated.

- options.lba_size_set adjusts the number of the LBA size set during some statistics. Each LBA range will be calculated as the total LBA/the number of sets.

The following is a sample configuration:

```
% batch_analysis.m
ptions.export_report=1;
if exist('name','var')
    options.report_name=[name, '_raw.ppt'];
else
    options.report_name='trace_analysis_raw.ppt';
end

% report title
if options.export_report
    saveppt2(options.report_name,'f',0,'t',...
        [' Basic Workload Analysis Report'])
    options.plot_figure=1;
end
```

```
options.plot_fontsize=10;
options.offset_time=0; [lists_action,idx]=sortrows(lists_
action,1); lists_cmd=lists_cmd(idx,:);
```

After the simple setting, it starts to call all of the analysis functions. The analyzed data is saved for further usage, such as generating a PowerPoint analysis report.

```
%% call individual sub-functions
%0 get the very basic workload information
basic_info=sub_basic_info(lists_action,lists_cmd,options);

%1 average queue depth for completion and arrival
queue_record=sub_queue_depth(lists_action,lists_cmd,options);

%2 calculate the busy time of the device;
time_record=sub_busy_time(lists_action,options);

%3 average IOPS  and  throughput of requests options.
time_interval=1; % set the time window = 1s
average_record=sub_iops(lists_action,lists_cmd,options);


options.time_interval=6; % set the time window = 6s
average_record= sub_iops(lists_action,lists_cmd,options);

%4 calcuate the size distribution
req_size_record=sub_size_dist(lists_action,lists_cmd,options);

%5 calcuate the LBA/size  distribution
options.lba_size_set=50; % adjust the range of LBA  in
plotting
lba_stat_array=sub_lba_dist(lists_action,lists_cmd,options);
```

```
%6 sequential analysis (stream/commands/size/queue  length)
options.near_sequence=0;  % sequential analysis
options.S2_threshold =32; % limit the minimum number which is
counted as sequence stream
options.max_stream_length=1024;
options.seq_size_threshold=1024; % the size constraint for a
sequential stream
sequence_stat=sub_sequence_analysis(lists_action,lists_cmd,
options);

options.near_sequence=1;  % near sequential analysis;
options.S2_threshold =32; % limit the minimum number which is
counted as sequence stream
options.S2_threshold2   =64; options.max_stream_length=1024;
options.seq_size_threshold=1024; % the size constraint for a
near sequential stream
sequence_stat=sub_sequence_analysis(lists_action,lists_
cmd,options);

%7 calculate the sequence queue
% sub_sequence_queue(lists_cmd,options)

%8 stack distance analysis - WOW
% options.spec_stack=[10,20,30];
% specify the stack distance for very large datasets;
stack_wow_record=sub_stack_wow(lists_cmd,options);

%9 stack distance analysis - ROW
stack_row_record=sub_stack_row(lists_cmd,options);

%10 frequented write update ratio - WOW options.access_type=0;
freq_wow_record=sub_freq_wow(lists_cmd,options);
```

```
%11 timed/ordered update ratio - WOW
options.access_type=0; time_wow_record=sub_time_wow(lists_
cmd,options);

%12 seek distance calcuation
seek_dist_record=sub_seek_dist(lists_cmd,options);

%13 queue length and idle time
idle_queue_record=sub_idle_queue(lists_action,options);

save analyzed_data
```

batch generate ppt.m specifies the analysis contents. First, it needs a PowerPoint template, like workload.pptx. This template has some predefined frames/layouts with specified names via a master page. Here you use the tool named exportTopptx[2] to access the slides:

```
options.ppt_template='E:\_workload.pptx';
exportToPPTX('open',options.ppt_template);


%% See all available masters and layout templates
% You can programmatically access master/layout information
% You can also run exportToPPTX by itself to have this
information printed to command window
pptxInfo = exportToPPTX;
fprintf('All_available_layout_templates:\n');
for ilayout=1:numel(pptxInfo.master(1).layout)
    fprintf('\t%d._%s\n',ilayout,pptxInfo.master(1).
    layout(ilayout).name);
end
```

---

[2]This tool is developed by Stefan Slonevskiy and downloaded from www.mathworks.com/matlabcentral/fileexchange/40277-exporttopptx

Second, it finds the corresponding analyzed results and figures from the saved dataset generated by batch analysis.m and creates the necessary remarks for the figures. Finally, it outputs a report in a pptx format. Take the IOPS page as an example. In this example, you use the predefined slide layout called 3Figure1Text, where there are some objects like Title 1, Footer Placeholder 2, Picture_11, Picture_12, Picture_22, and Text_main. These objects can be manipulated via the function exportToPPTX so you can easily adjust the content of the report based on requirements.

```
%% generate iops
filenames1=dir('iops*.fig');
filenames2=dir('throughput*.fig'); filenames3=dir
('reqsize*.fig');
% Layout #11: 3Figure1Text (Title 1, Footer Placeholder 2,
Picture_11, Picture_12, Picture_22, Text_
a1=size(filenames1,1);
for i=1:a1
    exportToPPTX('addslide','Layout','3Figure1Text');
    exportToPPTX('addtext','Estimated IOPS and Throughput','
    Position','Title');
    exportToPPTX('addtext','Basic Properties','Position',
    'Text_sup');
    for j=1:3
        eval(['filenames=filenames',int2str(j),';']);
        h = hgload(filenames(i).name);
        set(gcf, 'color', 'white');
        set(gca, 'color', 'none');
        pic_pos=['Picture_' int2str(j)];
        exportToPPTX('addpicture',h,'Position',
        pic_pos,'Scale','maxfixed');
        close(h);
```

```
end
temp_str1='Observe_if_burst_and_idleness_exist';
temp_str2='Bursts_exist_if_there_are_peaks_much_
higher_than_the_average';
temp_str3='Idleness_exist_if_there_are_troughs_much_
lower_than_the_average';
```

A sample of the auto-generated presentation slide is shown in Figures A-1 and A-2. The users can easily adjust the slide layouts for their scenarios.

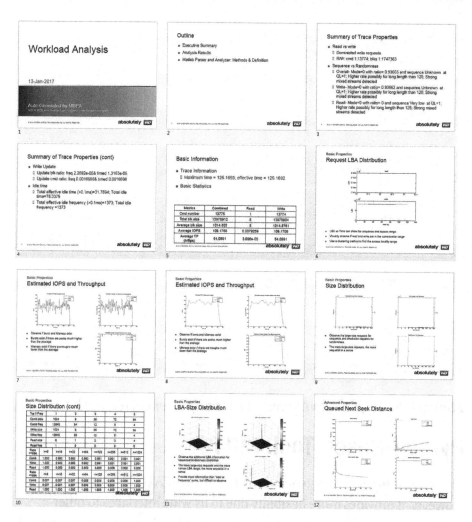

Figure A-1. *A generated PowerPoint sample report*

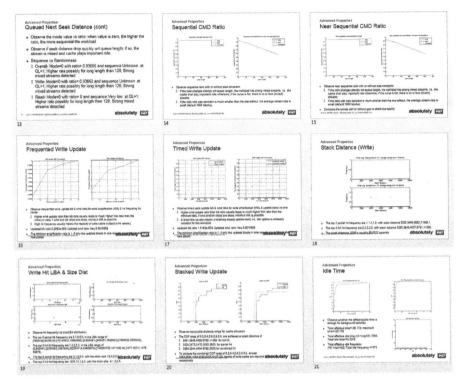

Figure A-2. *A generated PowerPoint sample report (cont'd)*

Python-Based Tool: PBPAR

The Python-based tool is generally similar to the MATLAB-based tool. However, it provides more flexibility due to its wide interfaces to other programming languages. In addition, it is completed free and open sourced.

The following code shows how to call the analysis functions:

```
from numpy import *
from matplotlib.pylab import *
from scipy.stats import *
from scipy import *
import dill
from PBPAR import *
```

```
lists_action=lists_action[:,0:2]
options=options_class()
options.export_report = 0
options.report_name = 'trace_analysis.ppt' options.export_
report = 0
options.plot_fontsize = 10
options.time_interval = 50
options.plot_figure = 1
options.offset_time = 0

idx=argsort(lists_action[:,0])
lists_cmd=lists_cmd[ix_(list(idx),[0,1,2])]
lists_action=lists_action[ix_(list(idx),[0,1])]

#0 obtain basic information
basic_info=sub_basic_info(lists_action,lists_cmd,options)

### call individual sub-functions

#1 average queue depth for completion and arrival
queue_record=sub_queue_depth(lists_action,lists_cmd,options)

#2 calculate the device busy time;
time_record=sub_busy_time(lists_action,options)

#3 average IOPS and throughput of requests
options.time_interval = 1
average_record=sub_iops(lists_action,lists_cmd,options)
options.time_interval = 6
average_record=sub_iops(lists_action,lists_cmd,options)

#4 calculate the size distribution req_size_record=sub_size_
dist(lists_action,lists_cmd,options)
```

```
#5 calculate  the  LBA/size  distribution
options.lba_size_set  =  50
lba_stat_array=sub_lba_dist(lists_action,lists_cmd,options)

#6 sequential analysis (stream/commands/size/queue    length)
options.near_sequence = 0
options.S2_threshold = 32
options.S2_threshold2 = 64
options.max_stream_length = 1024
options.seq_size_threshold = 1024 sequence_stat=sub_sequence_
analysis(lists_action,lists_cmd,options)

options.near_sequence = 1
options.S2_threshold = 32
options.S2_threshold2 = 64
options.max_stream_length = 1024
options.seq_size_threshold = 1024 sequence_stat=sub_sequence_
analysis(lists_action,lists_cmd,options)

#7 sequence queue analysis
## sub_sequence_queue(lists_cmd,options)

#8 stack distance analysis - WOW
#  options.spec_stack=[10,20,30]; # for very large dataset
stack_wow_record=sub_stack_wow(lists_cmd,options)

#9 stack distance analysis - ROW stack_row_record=sub_stack_
row(lists_cmd,options)

#10 frequented write update ratio - WOW
options.access_type = 0 freq_wow_record=sub_freq_wow(lists_
cmd,options)
```

```
#11 timed/ordered update ratio - WOW
options.access_type  =  0 time_wow_record=sub_time_wow(lists_
cmd,options)
```

```
#12  seek  distance  calcuation seek_dist_record=sub_seek_
dist(lists_cmd,options)
```

```
#13 queue length and idle time idle_queue_record=sub_idle_
queue(lists_action,options)
```

Finally, you can call `batch generate ppt.py` to create the slide similar to the MATLAB code. Note that you use the Python library python-pptx[3] as the wrapper to create the ppt file. python-pptx doesn't need a PowerPoint installation.

Interaction Between MATLAB and Python

Due to the similarity, it is not very difficult to convert code between two languages. Here are some tools/links for reference; Table A-1 compares them briefly:

- Small Matlab to Python compiler (SMOP): Converts MATLAB/Octave code to Python code, `https://github.com/victorlei/smop`

- LiberMate: A MATLAB-to-Python (SciPy/NumPy) translator, `https://github.com/awesomebytes/libermate`

- OMPC: Open-source MATLAB-to-Python compiler, which is a bit outdated, although partially functional, `ompc.juricap.com/`

---

[3]`http://python-pptx.readthedocs.io/en/latest/`

Table A-1. *Comparison of Code Converters*

	Developers	First / Latest	Required Library	Remarks
libermate	Eric C. Schug	March 2009/ May 2014	Numpy, scipy, matcompat	Imported libs are common
SMOP	Victor Lei	June 2013/ Dec 2016	smop	Supports Octave
OMPC	Peter Jurica	2008/ June 2010	ompc	Provides online version

Pylab of Python provides functions to read MATLAB mat files. Wrappers and interfaces between two languages are also available:

- pymatlab: Interfaces and communicates with MATLAB from Python. Users can easily integrate a project with a large MATLAB codebase into Python scripts by using MATLAB scripts as a part of the Python program. https://pypi.python.org/pypi/pymatlab.

- Python-Matlab wormholes: Allows both directions of interaction. However, only n-dimensional float arrays of data types are supported. https://github.com/pp5311006/python-matlab-wormholes.

- Python-Matlab Bridge: Offers the matlab magic extension for iPython to execute normal MATLAB code from within iPython. Scipy is required to handle sparse arrays. https://github.com/arokem/python-matlab-bridge.

- PyMat & pymat2: Allows Python programs to start, close, and communicate with a MATLAB engine session. The code is out of date. `pymat.sourceforge.net/`, `https://github.com/tinkuge/pymat2`

- mlabwrap, mlabwrap-purepy: Makes MATLAB look like a normal Python library using PyMat. `mlabwrap.sourceforge.net/`.

- pymex: Embeds the Python interpreter in MATLAB extension module. `https://github.com/kw/pymex`.

- matpy: Calls Python from MATLAB. Users can access MATLAB in multiple ways, such as creating variables or manipulating .mat files. `https://github.com/invenia/matpy`.

APPENDIX B

Blktrace and Tools

Blktrace was developed by Jens Axboe in early 2000. Since Linux version 2.617-rc1, it has been embedded into the kernel. In fact, there have been no major changes since 2007. It has some main features as follows:

- Low overhead, such as <0.5% CPU usage of one core in Intel E5-1620

- An easy-to-use configuration with simple CLI commands

- Highly configurable with trace IO on one or several devices, plus user-selectable filter events

- Low cost. Compared to a hardware bus analyzer, it's free of charge.

- Live and playback tracing

Figure B-1 shows the simplified structure of blktrace. You can see that it only considers device access after OS/FS cache. When IO enters to block IO layer (request queue), the relay channel per CPU gets events emitted, and blktrace then captures the events from the channels. Some events traces are listed as follows:

- Q: Request queue entry allocated

- S: Sleep during request queue allocation

© Jun Xu 2018
J. Xu, *Block Trace Analysis and Storage System Optimization*,
https://doi.org/10.1007/978-1-4842-3928-5

- I: Request queue insertion

- M: Back merge of IO on request queue

- F: Front merge of IO on request queue

- T: Unplug due to timer

- D: Request issued to underlying block dev

- C: Request completed

- P: Request queue plug operation

- U: Request queue unplug operation

- B: IO bounce operation

- X: IO split operation

- A: IO remap: MD or DM

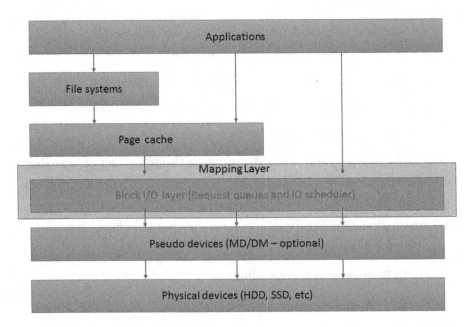

Figure B-1. *Blktrace structure*

It has wide applications, e.g.,:

- To analyze productivity of block devices (both real and virtual) and various hardware configurations

- To calculate potential expenses of resources (for example, at connection of program RAID)

- To define an optimal configuration for a specific program surrounding

- To estimate productivity of various file systems (e.g., EXT4, JFS, XFS, Btrfs) via differently interaction with block subsystems

- To analyze the efficiency of more complex systems, such as hybrid system, deduplication system, mobile storage system (e.g., Android), cloud system, etc.

Therefore, this tool has been extensively used in both academics and industries.

- Industry: HP, Oracle, IBM, Intel, WDC, Seagate, Huawei, Taobao, DHT, SGI, etc.

- Academics: Harvard University, University of California, Berkley, Imperial College of London, University of New South Wales, Florida International University, Sungkyunkwan University, Stony Brook University, University of Minnesota Twin Cities, Seoul National University, University of British Columbia, University of Maine, etc.

Some examples are listed as follows:

- Alibaba/Taobao: Debug an broken output pipe problem in the new kernel 2.6.37 and monitor performance for HDFS, `https://kernel.googlesource.com/pub/scm/linux/kernel/git/axboe/blktrace/9bf422b17cb2330f94376f8ca82a6e6cc496f9a3`.

- IBM: Monitor and tune virtual I/O scheduler for virtualized storage systems, `http://dl.acm.org/citation.cfm?id=1254826`.

- Intel: Aid tool for Hystor (a high-performance hybrid storage system, SSD+HDD) design, `http://dl.acm.org/citation.cfm?id=1995902`.

- University of California, Berkeley: Determine the proper chunk size in HDFS for shared storage systems, `www.eecs.berkeley.edu/alspaugh/papers/cake socc 2012.pdf`.

- University of Maine: Aid tool for migration algorithm design for hybrid storage systems, `http://web.eece.maine.edu/jyue/papers/mascots11.pdf`.

Blktrace has a simple user interface. Two typical usages are

- **Without command filter**

  ```
  $ blktrace -d /dev/sda -o blktrace.sda
  ```

- **With command filter**

  ```
  $ blktrace -d /dev/sda -a fs -o - |blkparse -i -
  ```

The results can be output to the terminal, HDD, RAM disk, or TMPFS. It may be better to store trace in a different device from the one traced. The command details can be found in its man page or you can refer to the user manual.

The trace collected by blktrace is in a binary format. In order to convert into a readable format, you need some tools to parse it. Blkparse produces formatted output of event streams of block devices. Figure B-2 provides an example output by blktrace. You can see that the IO request to device generally has D time (the time when request enters device) and C time (the time when request is completed), as well as some other file system-related time, such as queuing, insert, and merge.

Dev ID	CPU	Sequence number	Timestamp	PID	Event	IO	Start block + number of blocks And [process name]
8,16	5	1	0.000000000	18615	A	R	1444645666 + 256 <- (8,17) 1444645632
8,16	5	2	0.000001850	18615	Q	R	1444645666 + 256 [java]
8,16	5	3	0.000006438	18615	G	R	1444645666 + 256 [java]
8,16	5	4	0.000008750	18615	P	N	[java]
8,16	5	5	0.000009980	18615	I	R	1444645666 + 256 [java]
8,16	5	0	0.000012990	0	m	N	cfq18615S / insert_request
...							
8,16	5	0	0.000028858	0	m	N	cfq18615S / dispatch_insert
8,16	5	0	0.000030888	0	m	N	cfq18615S / dispatched a request
8,16	5	0	0.000031648	0	m	N	cfq18615S / activate rq, drv=1
8,16	5	6	0.000031865	18615	D	R	1444645666 + 256 [java]
8,16	5	7	0.000046560	18615	U	N	[java] 1
...							
8,16	5	14	0.000118208	18615	D	R	1444645922 + 256 [java]
8,16	5	15	0.000356669	0	C	R	1444645666 + 256 [0]
8,16	5	0	0.000367525	0	m	N	cfq18615S / complete rqnoidle 0
8,16	5	0	0.000369042	0	m	N	cfq18615S / set_slice=100
8,16	1	1	0.000656835	0	C	R	1444645922 + 256 [0]

Figure B-2. *A sample trace collected by blktrace and parsed by blkparse*

There are other tools related to blktrace:

- Verify blkparse/blkrawverify verifies an output file from blkparse.

- Btrace calls blktrace on the specified devices and pipes the output through blkparse for formatting.

- Btt represents an abbreviation of the expression of the blktrace timeline that is possible to translate as the chronicle of blktrace, www.fis.unipr.it/doc/ blktrace-1.0.1/btt.pdf.

- Seekwatcher generates graphs from blktrace to visualize IO patterns and performance, https://oss.oracle.com/mason/seekwatcher/.

- Iowatcher graphs the results of a blktrace run, masoncoding.com/iowatcher/.

These tools generally provide some basic information about the trace properties. For example, Seekwatcher visualizes some basic metrics such as throughput and IOPS, as shown in Figure B-3. Iowatcher makes an animation of IO events. However, they do not provide any inside information related to cache and queue, which is particularly useful for the new generation disk drives, like SMR. This motivates the development of a dedicated tool for block-level trace analysis.

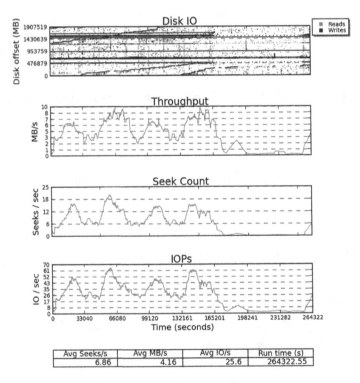

Figure B-3. *Basic information by IOwatcher*

Bibliography

[1] R. Gastaldi and G. Campardo, Eds., *In Search of the Next Memory: Inside the Circuitry from the Oldest to the Emerging Non-Volatile Memories*. Springer, 2017.

[2] M. Xie, L. Xia, and J. Xu, "State-dependent m/g/1/k queuing model for hard disk drives," *IEEE CASE (the 13th Conference on Automation Science and Engineering)*, Xian, China, Mar 2017.

[3] J. Niu, J. Xu, and L. Xie, "Optimal selection of garbage collection dirty threshold to balance power consumption and space release," *IEEE CAC*, China, Oct 2017.

[4] A. Amer, J. Holliday, D. Long, E. Miller, J. Paris, and T. Schwarz, "Data management and layout for shingled maganetic recording," in *IEEE trans. Magnetics*, vol. 47, no. 10, pp. 3691–3697, 2011.

[5] T. Feldman and G. Gibson, "Shingled magetic recording: areal density increase requires new data management," *USENIX; Login*, vol. 38, no. 3, pp. 22–30, 2013.

[6] J. Niu, M. Xie, J. Xu, L. Xie, and L. Xia, "Smr drive performance analysis under different workload environments," *Control Engineering Practice*, vol. 75, pp. 86–97, 2018.

© Jun Xu 2018
J. Xu, *Block Trace Analysis and Storage System Optimization*,
https://doi.org/10.1007/978-1-4842-3928-5

[7] J. Niu, J. Xu, and L. Xie, "A deep look at smr performance via simulation approach," *IEEE ICCA (13th International conference on control and automation)*, Ohrid, Macedonia, Jul 2017.

[8] ——, "Analytical modeling of smr drive under different workload environments," *IEEE ICCA (13th International conference on control and automation)*, Ohrid, Macedonia, Jul 2017.

[9] E. Brewer and L. Ying, "Disks for data centers," *File system and storage technology (FAST)*, CA, USA, 2016.

[10] Y. Shiroishi, K. Fukuda, I. Tagawa, H. Iwasaki, S. Takenoiri, H. Tanaka, H. Mutoh, and N. Yoshikawa, "Future options for hdd storage," *IEEE TRANS. MAGNETICS*, vol. 45, no. 10, pp. 3816–3822, 2009.

[11] C. F. Adams and C. R. McKie, "Balanced actuator which accesses separate disc assemblies," Seagate, Patent US6115215A, 1998.

[12] E. Kim, "Ssd performance - a primer: An intrduction to solid state drive performance, evaluation and test," SNIA, Tech. Rep., 2013.

[13] B. Schroeder and G. A. Gibson, "Disk failures in the real world: What does an mttf of 1,000,000 hours mean to you?" *The 5th USENIX conference on File and Storage Technologies*, Oct 2007.

[14] J. Meza, Q. Wu, S. Kumar, and O. Mutlu, "A large-scale study of flash memory failures in the field," *ACM Sigmetrics*, Portland, OR, USA, 2015.

[15] J. Niu, J. Xu, and L. Xie, "Hybrid storage systems: A survey of architectures and algorithms," *IEEE Access*, vol. 6, pp. 13 385–13 406, 2018.

[16] J. R. David Reinsel, "Breaking the 15K-rpm HDD Performance Barrier with Solid State Hybrid Drives," 2013.

[17] M. K. Qureshi, V. Srinivasan, and J. A. Rivers, "Scalable high performance main memory system using phase-change memory technology," *ACM SIGARCH Computer Architecture News*, vol. 37, no. 3, pp. 24–33, 2009.

[18] Y. Huai, "Spin-transfer torque MRAM (STT-MRAM): Challenges and prospects," *AAPPS Bulletin*, vol. 18, no. 6, pp. 33–40, 2008.

[19] H.-S. P. Wong, H.-Y. Lee, S. Yu, Y.-S. Chen, Y. Wu, P.-S. Chen, B. Lee, F. T. Chen, and M.-J. Tsai, "Metal–oxide RRAM," *Proceedings of the IEEE*, vol. 100, no. 6, pp. 1951–1970, 2012.

[20] B. Jacob, S. W. Ng, and S. Rodriguez, *Memory Systems: Cache, DRAM, Disk*, Elsevier, 2008.

[21] D. Lee, M. O'Sullivan, and C. Walker, "Measurement for improving the design of commodity archival storage tiers," *Utility and Cloud Computing (UCC), 2011 Fourth IEEE International Conference*. IEEE, 2011, pp. 275–280.

[22] I. Koltsidas, S. Sarafijanovic, M. Petermann,
N. Haustein, H. Seipp, R. Haas, J. Jelitto, T. Weigold,
E. Childers, D. Pease *et al.*, "Seamlessly integrating
disk and tape in a multi-tiered distributed file
system," *2015 IEEE 31st International Conference on
Data Engineering*. IEEE, 2015, pp. 1328–1339.

[23] N. Muppalaneni and K. Gopinath, "A multi-tier
RAID storage system with RAID1 and RAID5,"
*Parallel and Distributed Processing Symposium,
2000. IPDPS 2000. Proceedings. 14th International*.
IEEE, 2000, pp. 663–671.

[24] Wikipedia, "Flash memory — Wikipedia, the free
encyclopedia," 2017. [Online]. Available: "https://
en.wikipedia.org/wiki/Flash memory"

[25] H.-S. P. Wong, S. Raoux, S. Kim, J. Liang, J. P.
Reifenberg, B. Rajendran, M. Asheghi, and K. E.
Goodson, "Phase change memory," *Proceedings of
the IEEE*, vol. 98, no. 12, pp. 2201–2227, 2010.

[26] K. A. Bailey, P. Hornyack, L. Ceze, S. D. Gribble, and
H. M. Levy, "Exploring storage class memory with
key value stores," *Proceedings of the 1st Workshop on
Interactions of NVM/FLASH with Operating Systems
and Workloads*, ACM, 2013, p. 4.

[27] C. W. Smullen, J. Coffman, and S. Gurumurthi,
"Accelerating enterprise solid-state disks with
non-volatile merge caching," *Green Computing
Conference, 2010 International*, IEEE, 2010,
pp. 203–214.

[28]   N. Lu, I.-S. Choi, S.-H. Ko, and S.-D. Kim, "A PRAM based block updating management for hybrid solid state disk," *IEICE Electronics Express*, vol. 9, no. 4, pp. 320–325, 2012.

[29]   M. Tarihi, H. Asadi, A. Haghdoost, M. Arjomand, and H. Sarbazi-Azad, "A hybrid non-volatile cache design for solid-state drives using comprehensive I/O characterization," *IEEE Transactions on Computers*, vol. 65, no. 6, pp. 1678–1691, 2016.

[30]   G. Sun, Y. Joo, Y. Chen, Y. Chen, and Y. Xie, "A hybrid solid-state storage architecture for the performance, energy consumption, and lifetime improvement," *Emerging Memory Technologies*, Springer, 2014, pp. 51– 77.

[31]   W. Xiao, H. Dong, L. Ma, Z. Liu, and Q. Zhang, "HS-BAS: A hybrid storage system based on band awareness of Shingled Write Disk," *Computer Design (ICCD), 2016 IEEE 34th International Conference on*, IEEE, 2016, pp. 64–71.

[32]   P. Petriuk, "Openstack architecture," Mirantis, White paper, 2014.

[33]   S. A. Weil, S. A. Brandt, E. L. Miller, D. D. E. Long, and C. Maltzahn, "Ceph: A scalable, high-performance distributed file system," *Proceedings of the 7th Conference on Operating Systems Design and Implementation (OSDI 06)*, 2006.

[34]   K. Singh, *Learning Ceph*. Packt Publishing, 2015.

[35]   D. G. Feitelson, *Workload Modeling for Computer Systems Performance Evaluation*, UK: Cambridge University Press, 2014.

[36]   R. Nou, J. Giralt, and T. Cortes, "Automatic i/o scheduler selection through online workload analysis," in *Ubiquitous Intelligence & Computing and 9th International Conference on Autonomic & Trusted Computing (UIC/ATC)*, Fukuoka, Japan, 2012.

[37]   Y. Chen, "Workload-driven design and evaluation of large-scale data-centric systems," PhD thesis, UC Berkeley, 2012. [Online]. Available: `http://www.eecs.berkeley.edu/Pubs/TechRpts/2012/EECS-2012-73.pdf`.

[38]   L. K. John and A. M. G. Maynard, Eds., *Workload Characterization of Emerging Computer Applications*, Springer Science+Business Media, LLC, 2001.

[39]   W. W. Hsu and A. J. Smith, "Characteristics of i/o traffic in personal computer and server workloads," *IBM Sysms Journal*, vol. 42, no. 2, p. 347, 2003.

[40]   Q. M. Le, K. SathyanarayanaRaju, A. Amer, and J. Holliday, "Workload impact on shingle write disks: all-writes can be alright," in *19th IEEE ISMASCTS*, Jul 2011, pp. 444 – 446.

[41]   B. Gregg, *Systems Performance: Enterprise and the Cloud*, Prentice Hall, 2013.

[42]   A. Riska and E. Riedel, "Disk drive level workload characterization," *Annual Tech 06: USENIX Annual Technical Conference*, 2006.

[43] V. T. Priya Sehgal and E. Zadok, "Evaluating performance and energy in file system server workloads," *File system and storage technologies*, 2010.

[44] A. Williams, M. Arlitt, C. Williamson, and K. Barker, *Web Information Systems Engineering and Internet Technologies Book Series*, 2005, vol. 2, ch. WEBWORKLOAD CHARACTERIZATION: TEN YEARS LATER, pp. 3–21.

[45] R. Eigenmann, Ed., *Performance Evaluation and Benchmarking with Realistic Applications*, The MIT Press, 2001.

[46] S. Klyaus, *Dynamic Tracing with DTrace & SystemTap*, online book, http://myaut.github.io/dtrace-stap-book/.

[47] B. Gregg, *DTrace: Dynamic Tracing in Oracle Solaris, Mac OS X and FreeBSD*, Oracle, 2011.

[48] Wikipedia, "Cache replacement policies — Wikipedia, the free encyclopedia," 2017.

[49] L. Cherkasova, *Improving WWW proxies performance with greedy-dual-size-frequency caching policy*, Hewlett-Packard Laboratories, 1998.

[50] E. J. O'neil, P. E. O'neil, and G. Weikum, "The lru-k page replacement algorithm for database disk buffering," *ACM SIGMOD Record*, vol. 22, no. 2, pp. 297–306, 1993.

[51] S. Jin and A. Bestavros, "Popularity-aware greedy dual-size web proxy caching algorithms," *Distributed computing systems, 2000. Proceedings. 20th international conference on*, IEEE, 2000, pp. 254–261.

[52] A. Traeger, E. Wright, N. Joukov, and C. P. Wright, "A nine year study of file system and storage benchmarking," *ACM trans. storage*, vol. 4, no. 2, p. 5, 2009.

[53] SPC, *SPC BENCHMARK 1C*, 1st ed., Storage Performance Council, CA, USA, Nov 2012.

[54] J. S. Bucy, J. Schindler, S. W. Schlosser, and G. R. Ganger, *The DiskSim Simulation environment version 4.0 reference manual*, Carnegie Mellon University, PA, USA, 2008.

[55] Futuremark, *PCMark: the complete benchmark*, 2nd ed., Futuremark, Apr 2016.

[56] H. Kim, S. Seshadri, C. L. Dickey, and L. Chiu, "Evaluating phase change memory for enterprise storage systems: A study of caching and tiering approaches," *ACM Transactions on Storage (TOS)*, vol. 10, no. 4, p. 15, 2014.

[57] Y. Kim, A. Gupta, B. Urgaonkar, P. Berman, and A. Sivasubramaniam, "Hybridstore: A cost-efficient, high- performance storage system combining SSDs and HDDs," in *2011 IEEE 19th Annual International Symposium on Modelling, Analysis, and Simulation of Computer and Telecommunication Systems*, IEEE, 2011, pp. 227– 236.

[58] D. L. Moal, Z. Bandic, and C. Guyot, "Shingled file system host-side management of shingled magnetic recording disks," in *Consumer Electronics (ICCE), 2012 IEEE International Conference on*, 2012.

[59]   C. Jin, W.-Y. Xi, Z.-Y. Ching, F. Huo, and C.-T. Lim, "Hismrfs: a high performance file system for shingled storage array," *Mass Storage Systems and Technologies (MSST), 2014 30th Symposium on,* Santa Clara, CA, USA, 2014.

[60]   C. Li, D. Feng, Y. Hua, and F. Wang, "Improving RAID performance using an endurable SSD cache," *Parallel Processing (ICPP), 2016 45th International Conference on,* IEEE, 2016, pp. 396–405.

[61]   W. Liu, D. Feng, L. Zeng, and J. Chen, "Understanding the swd-based raid system," in *International Conference on Cloud Computing and Big Data,* 2014.

[62]   A. Thomasian and Y. Tang, "Performance, reliability, and performability of a hybrid raid array and a comparison with traditional raid1 arrays," *Cluster Computing,* vol. 15, pp. 239–253, 2012.

[63]   M. Li and J. Shu, "Daco: A high-performance disk architecture designed specially for large-scale erasure-coded storage systems," *IEEE TRANSACTIONS ON COMPUTERS,* vol. 59, no. 10, pp. 1350–1362, 2010.

[64]   D. A. Patterson, G. Gibson, and R. H. Katz, "A case for redundant arrays of inexpensive disks (raid)," *The 1988 ACM SIGMOD International Conference on Management of Data,* 1988, pp. 109–116.

[65]   S. Wu, H. Jiang, L. Tian, and B. Mao, "Workout: Io workload outsourcing for boosting raid reconstruction performance," *7th USENIX Conference on File and Storage Technologies, FAST 09*, San Francisco, CA, 2009.

[66]   Z. Ren, X. Xu, J. Wan, W. Shi, and M. Zhou, "Workload analysis, implications, and optimization on a production hadoop cluster: A case study on taobao," *Services Computing, IEEE Trans. on*, vol. 7, no. 2, pp. 307 – 321, 2014.

[67]   G. Wang, A. R. Butt, H. Monti, and K. Gupta, "Towards synthesizing realistic workload traces for studying the hadoop ecosystem," *IEEE 19th MASCOTS*, 2011, pp. 400–408.

[68]   Y. Chen, S. Alspaugh, and R. H. Katz, "Design insights for mapreduce from diverse production workloads," UC Berkeley, http://www.eecs. berkeley.edu/Pubs/TechRpts/2012/EECS-2012- 17.pdf, Tech. Rep. UCB/EECS-2012- 17, Jan 2012.

[69]   B. Atikoglu, Y. Xu, E. Frachtenberg, S. Jiang, and M. Paleczny, "Workload analysis of a large-scale key-value store," *SIGMETRICS '12*, 2012, pp. 53–64.

[70]   J. Shafer, S. Rixner, and A. Cox, "The hadoop distributed filesystem: Balancing portability and performance," *Performance Analysis of Systems & Software (ISPASS)*, Mar 2010, pp. 122 – 133.

[71]   S. Kavulya, J. Tany, R. Gandhi, and P. Narasimhan, "An analysis of traces from a production mapreduce cluster," *10th IEEE/ACM International Conference on Cluster, Cloud and Grid Computing*, 2010, pp. 94–103.

[72] C. L. Abad, N. Robert, Y. Lu, and R. H. Campbell, "A storage-centric analysis of mapreduce workloads: File popularity, temporal locality and arrival patterns," *IEEE International Symposium on Workload Characterization (IISWC)*, 2012, pp. 100–109.

[73] K. Ren, Y. Kwon, M. Balazinska, and B. Howe, "Hadoops adolescence: A comparative workload analysis from three research clusters," Carnegie Mellon University, PA, USA, Tech. Rep. CMU-PDL-12-106, 2012.

[74] G. Wang, A. R. Butt, P. Pandey, and K. Gupta, "A simulation approach to evaluating design decisions in mapreduce setups," *IEEE/ACM MASCOTS*, London UK, Sep 2009.

[75] J. Axboe, *blktrace User Guide*, 2007. [Online]. Available: www.cse.unsw.edu.au/~aaronc/iosched/doc/blktrace.html.

[76] A. Brunelle, *Block Layer tracing: blktrace*, knfiu. mimuw.edu.pl, 2007.

[77] T. Harter, D. Borthakur, S. Dong, A. S. Aiyer, L. Tang, A. C. Arpaci-Dusseau, and R. H. Arpaci-Dusseau, "Analysis of hdfs under hbase: a facebook messages case study." *FAST*, 2014, pp. 199–212.

[78] C. Mason, *Seekwatcher*, Oracle, https://oss.oracle.com/mason/seekwatcher/.

[79] ——, *iowatcher*, 2013. [Online]. Available: masoncoding.com/iowatcher/

[80] S. A. Weil, "Ceph: Reliable, scalable, and high-performance distributed storage," Ph.D. dissertation, University of California, Santa Cruz, CA, USA, 2007.

[81] K. Singh, *Ceph Cookbook*. Packt Publishing, 2016.

[82] D. Gudu, M. Hardt, and A. Streit, "Evaluating the performance and scalability of the ceph distributed storage system," *IEEE International Conference on Big Data*, 2014, pp. 177–782.

[83] X. Zhang, S. Gaddam, and A. Chronopoulos, "Ceph distributed file system benchmarks on an openstack cloud," *IEEE International Conference on Cloud Computing in Emerging Markets (CCEM)*, Bangalore India, Nov 2015, pp. 113–120.

[84] F. Wang and M. Nelson, "Ceph parallel file system evaluation report," National Center for Computatational Sciences, OAK RIDGE NATIONAL LABORATORY, ORNL/TM-2013/151, 2013.

[85] S. Attaway, *A Practical Introduction to Programming and Problem Solving using Matlab*. Elsevier, 2013.

[86] M. Luiz, *Learning Python*. Sebastopol, CA: O'Reilly Media, 2013.

Index

© Jun Xu 2018
J. Xu, *Block Trace Analysis and Storage System Optimization*,
https://doi.org/10.1007/978-1-4842-3928-5

R

S

T, U

Printed in the United States
By Bookmasters